The church of God

The church of God

what it means to belong

Don Fortner

 EVANGELICAL PRESS

EVANGELICAL PRESS
12 Wooler Street, Darlington, Co. Durham, DL1 1RQ, England

© Evangelical Press 1991
First published 1991

British Library Cataloguing-in Publication Data available

ISBN 0 85234 281 0

Scripture quotations in this publication are from the Authorized (King James) Version.

Printed in Great Britain at the Bath Press, Bath, Avon.

Contents

1.
Public worship

'As for me, I will come into thy house in the multitude of thy mercy: and in thy fear will I worship toward thy holy temple' (Ps. 5:7)._

David, the man after God's own heart, found great pleasure and satisfaction in daily prayer and meditation. Daily, private, personal worship was a characteristic of his life. With the rising of the morning sun his heart was lifted up to God. Every morning he directed his prayer to the throne of grace and looked to his Lord with a heart of faith. Every evening he gave thanks to God and laid his head upon his pillow in the sweet rest of faith. That is the way to begin and end every day! Blessed is the man or woman who worships God in private. Let all who know and trust the living God worship him daily. Let all who follow Christ in the path of faith and obedience follow him also to the solitary place of private prayer. I would do everything within my power to promote and encourage private worship among the saints of God. Let every priest of God offer the daily sacrifices of prayer and praise to the Lord. But there is something even more important than private worship.

Does that last statement surprise you? I know that most people who are genuinely concerned for the glory of God and the worship of God rank personal, private worship above all things in the life of faith. But I am convinced that public worship, if it is true worship, is even more important than private worship.

David, the sweet singer of Israel, gave the highest possible regard to the matter of public worship. Without neglecting private worship, he said, 'As for me, I will come into thy house in the multitude of thy mercy: and in thy fear will I worship toward thy holy temple.' He could not force others to worship God, and would not if he could. 'But,' he says, 'as for me, I will come into thy house.' That is to say, 'I will come into the place of public worship in the assembly of God's saints, to worship the Lord my God.' And when he came into the place of worship with the saints of God, David was determined truly to worship the Lord. He says, 'In thy fear will I worship toward thy holy temple.' David was resolved in his heart, at every appointed time, to come with God's saints into the place of public worship, so that he might worship God in heaven, in the temple of his holiness. Let us look at this text a little more closely, and ask the Spirit of God to apply it to our hearts, so that David's words may become the expression of our own hearts' resolve.

'*I will come into thy house.*' The house of God is the congregation of the saints, wherever they gather in public assembly to worship God.

'I will come into thy house *in the multitude of thy mercy.*' It is not enough merely to 'go to church'. We must come into the house of God in faith, trusting the Lord's mercy. And there are a multitude of mercies with God in Christ. Sinners need mercy. We must come to the place of public worship as sinners trusting God's abundant mercy in Christ. If we do not come as sinners seeking mercy, we will not worship. But sinners looking to Christ for mercy always find a multitude of mercy in him (Luke 18:13-14). In him we find:

> Everlasting, covenant mercy (Jer. 31:31-34)
> Sin-atoning, redeeming mercy (Rom. 3:24-26)
> Effectual, saving mercy (Micah 7:18-20)
> Immutable, preserving mercy (Mal. 3:6)
> Daily, providential mercy (Rom. 8:28)

Truly, 'It is of the Lord's mercies that we are not consumed, because his compassions fail not' (Lam. 3:22), and every worshipper in God's house finds it to be so.

'*And in thy fear will I worship toward thy holy temple.*' We must come to the house of God with reverence and godly fear to worship him, that is, to see him, to hear him, to adore him, to praise him and to obey him. This was David's resolve. May it ever be yours and mine. May God give us grace to make public worship our delight and truly to worship him in the assembly of his saints.

In this chapter I want us to see five things about public worship, some of which will be dealt with in much more detail in later chapters.

1. Public worship is the single most important aspect of the believer's life

When David was banished from Jerusalem, the place of public worship, he envied even the sparrows who made their nests in the house of God. His heart longed not for the throne, the riches, or the power that had been taken from him, but for the assembly of God's saints in public worship. When the blessed privilege of public worship was taken from him for a short time, nothing was more important or precious to God's child (Ps. 84:1-4).

The fact is, all who are born of God love the assembly of God's saints in public worship and love the ministry of the gospel. There are no exceptions. God's people will not willingly absent themselves from the worship of God. It is true, there are many who very strictly attend, and even love, the outward service of public worship, who do not know the Lord. Their outward worship is nothing but a show of hypocrisy, for they never worship God in private. But anyone who wilfully neglects and despises the public assembly of the saints for worship, also neglects and despises private worship. And those who do not worship God do not know God.

Many people are very busy with all kinds of things. The cares and pleasures of life in this world consume almost all their time and attention. When it is convenient they attend church, give God a little tip and sing, 'Oh, how I love Jesus!' But any time something more important comes up (a good football match, a special television show, a visiting relative, or a sick dog!), they absent themselves from the house of God with little regret. They say to themselves, 'I can always go to church next week. The Lord knows my heart.' Of that much you can be sure: the Lord does know our hearts, and he will judge us accordingly!

Those who are truly God's people love the house of God and the

worship of God. They arrange their lives around the worship of God.
Nothing ever comes up, over which they have control, to keep them
from the house of God. They see to it that when the saints of God
gather for worship, they are among them, unless their absence is
genuinely unavoidable. Their faithfulness in the matter of public
worship is much more than a matter of duty. It is their delightful
choice. Public worship is the single most important aspect of their
lives in this world. Nothing is more important to the children of God
in this world than the public assembly of the saints for worship; and
that public assembly of the saints for worship is the local church, the
congregation of the Lord, the house of God.

Why do God's people place such importance upon the public
worship of the local church? Here are five reasons.

1. *This is the place where God meets sinners in saving mercy*. It is
true that God uses personal witnessing, tracts, tapes, books and other
instruments of gospel instruction to call his elect to life and faith in
Christ, but generally God saves his sheep in the congregations of his
saints when they are gathered for worship (Acts 2:1, 37-41). Sinners
in need of mercy should seek mercy where mercy is always found
in great, overflowing abundance; and mercy is always found in the
house of God.

God's saints know themselves to be sinners in need of mercy;
so they come, with all their needs, to the house of mercy, seeking the
Lord.

2. *This is the place where our family gathers*. Every true local church
is a family of believers. When the church gathers for worship, it is
the gathering of our family for sweet and blessed fellowship in the
gospel. Family members need each other, comfort each other and
help each other, because they love each other.

3. *This is the place where the Lord Jesus Christ meets with his
people*. Our Saviour promised that, wherever his people gather in
his name, he would be with them (Matt. 18:20). To gather in Christ's
name is to gather by faith in his name, for the honour of his name and
to worship in his name. If only two or three gather to worship the Son
of God, he will meet with them. The old man, Simeon, found God's
salvation, the Lord Jesus Christ, in the temple, the appointed place
of public worship (Luke 2:25-32), and if we would see Christ we

must come with his saints when they gather in the place of public worship.

4. *This is the place where God deals with men.* Each local congregation of believers is the house and temple of the living God (1 Cor. 3:16-17; 1 Tim. 3:15). God reveals his glory, gives out his law, makes known his will, bestows his blessings and instructs his people in his temple, his church. It is in this place that God speaks to men by his Spirit through his Word.

In all ages the people of God have been known and identified by their public gatherings for worship. Wherever God has had a people in this world, he has had a congregation to worship him. Sheep are always found in flocks. The only sheep who are alone are either lost or sick. And God's elect are sheep. No matter how few, they have always gathered together in public worship. In the public assembly they bear public, united testimony to the world of their Saviour's grace and glory. As an assembled body of believers they strengthen, cheer, comfort, encourage, edify and help one another by prayer, praise and the preaching of the gospel.

From the beginning of the Bible to the end there is a clear line of succession in this matter of public worship. Cain and Abel came to worship God in a public assembly. Noah's first act after the flood was an act of public worship to celebrate God's saving grace. Wherever the patriarchs pitched their tents in days of old, they erected an altar for worship. Throughout the Mosaic economy, the Jew who did not worship God in the tabernacle or temple was cut off from the congregation. Throughout the book of Acts, wherever God's children were scattered by persecution, they soon gathered in public assemblies for the worship of God.

Public worship is one identifying mark of true believers. With David, every saved sinner is resolved to worship God, saying, 'As for me, I will come into thy house in the multitude of thy mercy: and in thy fear will I worship toward thy holy temple.' By this let everyone examine himself or herself. Those who willingly and habitually absent themselves from the worship of God do not know God. A person may be outwardly faithful to the church of God who does not know God, but no one is faithful to Christ who is not faithful in the public assembly of his church for worship.

5. *The neglect of public worship is the first step towards total*

apostasy (Heb. 10:23-31). Seldom do men and women turn away from Christ and the gospel of his grace suddenly. Usually the charms of the world take men by degrees, gradually. Apostasy is usually so gradual that those who forsake Christ do not even realize they have forsaken him. How many there are who never attend, or seldom attend, the worship of God, who yet foolishly presume they are children of God! But their continued forsaking of the assembly of God's saints is proof that they never really knew the Lord Jesus Christ in saving faith (1 John 2:19). Those who wilfully neglect the assembly of God's saints for public worship, though they know the truth of God, tread underfoot the Son of God, count the blood of the covenant a useless thing and despise the Spirit of grace (Heb. 10:25, 26, 29).

2. If we would truly worship God in our public assemblies, everything must be governed by the Word of God

Sadly, much of that which goes on in the churches today is a mere show of religion, and religious show is an abomination to God. I do not question the sincerity of most religious people, but sincerity in doing evil does not make the evil good. Our Lord says, 'In vain they do worship me, teaching for doctrines the commandments of men' (Matt. 15:9). Paul tells us that religious ritualism, ceremonialism, legalism and showmanship are nothing but 'a show of wisdom in will worship', not for the honour of God, but for 'the satisfying of the flesh'.

Many imagine that small details in the worship of God are insignificant; but in the house of God, nothing is insignificant. Surely David's mistake in bringing the ark of God to Jerusalem should teach us the necessity of strict obedience in the worship of our God (1 Chron. 13:1-4; 15:11-15). We cannot worship the Lord God unless we worship him according to the Word of truth (1 Tim. 3:14-15; 2 Tim. 3:16-17; John 4:24).

We must worship the one true and living God as he is revealed in the person and work of his Son, the Lord Jesus Christ (John 14:6). The glory of the triune God is seen nowhere but in the face of Jesus Christ (2 Cor. 4:6). Our worship of God must be in the Spirit, that is, by the aid and direction of the Holy Spirit and in our hearts. True worship is purely spiritual. It is inspired by the Spirit of God. It arises from and takes place in the heart. And we must worship God in accordance with the truth, with true, sincere hearts, according to the Word of truth. In a word, our worship of God must be simple, unadorned, unpretentious and spiritual.

Both in doctrine and in activity, every aspect of public worship must be in precise accordance with Holy Scripture. We have no right to omit any aspect of service to God that is plainly laid down as the ordinance of our Lord in the New Testament; and we have no right to bring anything into the house of God that is not plainly set forth in the New Testament.

3. In public worship certain things are essential

The Word of God does not lay down any distinct order of service for public worship that must be rigidly followed, and we must be careful to avoid mere religious ritualism and ceremonialism. Yet all things must be done decently and in order. We must do nothing without thoughtful prayer and preparation, and all that is done must be done for the glory of God. In the New Testament we see five things which are essential to public worship. These five things should be regularly maintained in the services of every local church.

Firstly, when believers come together for worship, they should be led in *united, public prayer* (1 Tim. 2:1). Secondly, every assembly for public worship should give attention to *the public reading of Holy Scripture* (1 Tim. 4:13; Rev. 1:3; Acts 15:30-31; Luke 4:16). Thirdly, *united, public praise, congregational singing*, is a blessed part of public worship (Eph. 5:19; Col. 3:16). Fourthly, the most important aspect of public worship is *the preaching of the gospel* (2 Tim. 4:1-2). Finally, we must regularly observe *the ordinances of our Lord* in public worship, that is, believers' baptism and the Lord's Supper.

Every service of every local church should be a worship service. Whether the congregation is many or few, whether it is gathered on Sunday morning, or in the middle of the week, when God's people gather in public assembly, they ought to be led in the worship of God by faithful, well-prepared, gospel-preaching pastors. Each service of the church should include prayer, reading of Scripture, praise to God and gospel preaching. And the services should frequently include the observance of our Lord's ordinances.

4. There are some things we must carefully avoid in our assemblies for public worship

There are many things going on in churches today throughout the world, even in some places where men claim to preach the gospel of God's free and sovereign grace in Christ, which have no place at all in the house of God. The house of God is a house of prayer, a house of worship, a centre for preaching. Any other function for the church is out of order. The church of God is not a political arena, an educational centre, or a social club. Any church that functions as such has missed her calling. But in our worship services themselves, there are four evils which we must studiously avoid.

We must avoid *showmanship and entertainment*. Any person interested in the glory of God knows that the church of God has no business involving itself with sporting events, bingo parties and such like; but there is a tendency, even with the most conscientious people, to use their gifts and talents to entertain people, rather than edify them.

Every form of *idolatry* must be studiously avoided. Crosses, robes, stained glass windows, religious pictures and symbols are not aids, but hindrances, to spiritual worship. Any use of physical objects in the worship of God is idolatry.

Ritualism must be carefully avoided. Any religious service, rite or ceremony not ordained of God is a meaningless ritual. Any superstitious service performed in the name of God, anything which claims to confer grace or spiritual benefit by means of an outward action, is a mockery of divine worship.

Another thing we must carefully avoid is *emotionalism*. The waving of hands, shouting, making religious gestures, etc. only calls attention to oneself. There is no place in the house of God for the exaltation of self. I do not mean to imply that worship is without emotion. True worship floods our hearts with many emotions. When Christ is preached, if God is gracious and the Holy Spirit applies the Word to our hearts, joy and sorrow, conviction and consecration, solemnity and gaiety, humility and exultation all, at the same time, may be found in the believer's heart; but deep, heartfelt emotions, if they are sanctified by God, do not show themselves in mere gestures and momentary outbursts of emotionalism. They show themselves in the effect they have upon our lives.

We do not come to the house of God to make a show of religion, to fulfil our religious obligation, or to get a shot of spiritual excitement. We come to the house of God to see, hear and worship God in Christ, for the comfort, strengthening and edification of our souls.

5. There are some tests by which our worship of God may be proved

If we truly worship God when we meet together in the house of God, our worship will be reflected in the effect it has upon us. An hour of religious excitement, no matter how deeply it is felt, is useless if it does not affect our lives. True worship affects a person's life. I offer these six tests by which to examine and prove all exercises in public and private worship.

1. *True worship reaches the heart and conscience.* False worship — mere ritualism or emotionalism — is like taking drugs. It has a gradually declining effect upon the heart, and people soon become immune to it. This is one reason why churches and religious leaders must always devise newer, bigger, more exciting programmes. But the worship of the living God never has a deadening effect. Men and women who worship in Spirit and truth drink from the same fountain year after year, with ever-increasing delight. The gospel of Christ never becomes mundane to them.

2. *True worship draws our hearts closer to Christ in sweet communion, faith, love and obedience.* The gospel of Christ shuts us up to Christ, shows us Christ and leaves us looking to Christ. This is always the work of the Holy Spirit (John 16:13-14). True worship is the continual reviving of the believer's heart by the Holy Spirit. It is the Spirit's knitting our own hearts to the Lord Jesus Christ.

3. *True worship causes the believer to grow in the grace and knowledge of Christ.* When the saints of God are fed with knowledge and understanding by the Spirit of God, through the preaching of the gospel, they grow in grace, mature in faith and increase in love. The worship of Christ is edifying.

4. *True worship affects the lives of God's people.* Those who

worship God, walk with God by faith; and walking with God affects the way a person thinks, talks and behaves at home, on the job and in the church. Mean-spirited, dishonest, slanderous men and women do not worship the living God.

5. *True worship inspires, increases and enlarges a believer's submission, consecration and dedication to the Lord Jesus Christ* (Rom. 12:1-2; 1 Cor. 6:19-20). The more a believer sees and knows of Christ's glorious person, redemptive work and heavenly exaltation, the more he desires to give himself entirely to his beloved Lord.

6. *True worship causes the believer to hope for, and anxiously anticipate, that blessed, endless day of perfect worship which we shall enjoy in heaven's glory.* Every time I am enabled, in some measure, to worship God, my heart is moved with excited hope to think of that eternity which awaits the saints of God, in which our lives, our very existence, will be so perfectly conformed to the image of Christ that we shall perfectly worship the Lord God at all times and in all things for ever! Truly, ours is a blessed hope!

   May God help each one of us, as long as we live upon the earth, to make David's determination the holy resolve of our own hearts: 'As for me, I will come into thy house in the multitude of thy mercy: and in thy fear will I worship toward thy holy temple.'

2.
The church of God

'Take heed therefore unto yourselves, and to all the flock, over the which the Holy Ghost hath made you overseers, to feed the church of God, which he hath purchased with his own blood' (Acts 20:28).

When John the Baptist cried, 'Behold the Lamb of God which taketh away the sin of the world,' and two of his disciples left him to follow the Lord Jesus Christ, something new was begun in the world. An entirely new bond was introduced into the world: a bond of love to Christ and to one another in him. And that bond of love is called 'the church of God'. It is true, the church universal, the mystical body and bride of Christ, includes all the saints of God from the beginning to the end of the world; but in the Old Testament the visible church of God was a national, political body. It was a physical family, comprised of men, women and children with a flesh and blood kinship. The church of the Old Testament was the nation of Israel, the seed of Abraham, a society of Jews. But a spiritual society, in which the only bond holding its members together is their relationship to their Master, the Lord Jesus Christ, was a totally new thing in John's day. The bond of the Old Testament church was flesh and blood and law. The bond of the church of the New Testament is faith and love and grace.

This society of believers, united to one another and to Christ by love and faith in him, is the church of the New Testament. Our English word 'church' means 'assembly', or 'congregation'. The Greek word from which it is translated is derived from a word which means 'that which belongs to the Lord'. The church of God in this world is a divine society, a congregation that belongs to God. It is the congregation of God's elect. This New Testament church began with our Lord's earthly ministry. It is built upon the apostolic confession and witness of Christ's life as our representative, death as our substitute, resurrection as our High Priest and ascension and exaltation as our Lord and King. On the Day of Pentecost the Holy Spirit fell upon the church of God at Jerusalem, filling it with power and sanctifying it as the kingdom of God in this world.

It is of the utmost importance that every child of God should know the purpose and value of the church of God in this world, and commit him or herself to it. The text which heads this chapter is taken from the book of Acts, and one great purpose of the book of Acts is to show us how God works in this world through his church. The book of Acts is the inspired record of the progress of the church during its first thirty years of ministry after the death of Christ. The most prominent figure in the church during those first thirty years was the apostle Paul, and it is this man, Paul, who is speaking in Acts 20:28. He is addressing the elders at Ephesus, giving them a solemn charge regarding their responsibilities as the servants of God. He says, 'Take heed therefore unto yourselves, and to all the flock, over the which the Holy Ghost hath made you overseers, to feed the church of God, which he hath purchased with his own blood.'

In this chapter I want to raise six very practical questions about the church of God and answer them from the Word of God.

1. What is the church of God?

The word 'church' is used in three ways in the New Testament.

1. It is used to describe *all true believers of all ages*, from the beginning of the world to its end, all the saints of the Old Testament and New Testament ages, all of God's elect upon the earth and in heaven. This is what we call the universal church. It is the mystical body and spiritual bride of the Lord Jesus Christ. It is that spiritual body of which Jesus Christ is the Head (Eph. 1:22; 5:23-27).

2. The word 'church' is used to describe *local, visible assemblies of professed believers in a given place*. In every local church there

are both believers and unbelievers, wheat and tares, sheep and goats, true possessors of faith and false professors of faith. Every local church has in its membership both the true and the false, but still every local assembly of men and women who profess faith in Christ and the gospel of God's free grace in him is set forth as a local church and is called 'the church of God' (Rom. 16:1-5).

3. The word 'church' is used to describe *all true churches at any given time in the world.* Obviously I do not suggest that the church of God is made up of all churches and denominations, but it does include all New Testament churches at any given time in the world. We are one in Christ, one in purpose, one in heart and one in desire. All true gospel churches in this world in Jesus Christ are one (1 Cor. 10:32; 12:28).

In Acts 20:28 the apostle Paul is addressing the elders of a particular local assembly at Ephesus, or perhaps elders from several local assemblies in the Ephesus area, but the words 'the church of God' in this text have reference to the local church. In this verse Paul tells us three things about the church of God, which are true of every local, gospel church.

1. *The church belongs to God.* The church which I pastor, Grace Baptist Church, is the 'church of God' at Danville, Kentucky. The building in which we meet is not the church of God, but the men and women who assemble in that building are. The church does not belong to the Baptist denomination, to the pastor, the deacons, or even the people. We belong to God exclusively. We are God's people and God's property. God chose us to be his people in sovereign election before the world began (2 Thess. 2:13-14), God redeemed us to himself by the precious blood of Jesus Christ, his dear Son, at Calvary (Titus 2:14), and God called us to himself by the irresistible power and grace of his Spirit in regeneration, creating spiritual life within us and giving us faith in Christ (Col. 1:12-14).

By our election, our redemption and our calling, we belong to God; and what I have said of the church of God in Danville, Kentucky, is true of all God's churches in this world. Though there are unbelievers among us, all who know God in Christ, assembled together anywhere in the world, are a local church, and that assembly is the church of God. Let all beware: he that harms God's church touches the apple of his eye (1 Cor. 3:17).

2. *The church of God is a flock of sheep.* It is called 'the flock' because it is made up of Christ's sheep. John Gill says, 'A church of Christ is compared to a flock of sheep, living in gospel order, folded together and feeding in the same pasture, attending the word and ordinances, under the care of shepherds appointed by Christ, the Chief Shepherd.' Before we were converted, we were as lost sheep going astray from God our Saviour (Isa. 53:6). After conversion God's saints are compared to sheep because they are meek, inoffensive, patient and totally dependent upon Christ, who is their Shepherd. Sheep, like us, are far from being perfect creatures. They are silly, ignorant, helpless, defenceless, straying, needy, dumb animals, who cannot even give birth alone. Therefore they need, and must have, shepherds, pastors, to care for them.

3. *The church of God was purchased by the blood of Jesus Christ, who is God.* It is 'the church of God, which he hath purchased with his own blood'. Here is one of many, almost casual, affirmations of the fact that Jesus Christ is himself God. The writers of the New Testament never attempt to prove the deity of Christ. They simply assume that all believers know that the man who died at Calvary is God. The one who purchased and owns the church is God himself.

So thorough and complete is the union of Christ's two natures in one glorious person that the two can never be separated. That one who died for our sins is God Almighty, our eternal Creator. The price of our ransom from the curse of the law was 'his own blood'. Nothing but the life-blood of one who is both God and man could suffice to redeem us.

Our redemption by Christ was accomplished by *a legal purchase.* He paid our debt; therefore we have no debt to pay. He satisfied justice for us; therefore justice has no claim against us. He was cursed for us; therefore there is no curse upon us. He was condemned in our place; therefore we cannot be condemned.

The death of Christ as our substitute was *a particular purchase.* He did not purchase all people. He purchased 'the church' of God, his elect, whom he loved with an everlasting love. Christ's death accomplished *a complete purchase.* When he cried, 'It is finished,' the work was fully done, the purchase was complete. There is nothing to be added by man to make the transaction complete.

Our Lord's purchase was also *an effectual purchase.* All whom he purchased with his blood he will call by his Spirit, save by his grace, cleanse with his Word and present in heaven in perfect holiness (Eph. 5:25-27).

2. What is the purpose of the church in this world?

Why did our Lord establish his church in this world? Why did the apostles gather believers into local churches in every city?

In 1 Timothy 3:15-16 the apostle Paul tells us that the church is 'the pillar and ground of the truth'. The church of God is not the source of truth. God alone is the source of truth. The church is not the foundation upon which truth is built. Christ is. We have no right to formulate, devise, or even shape the truth. That is not our prerogative. But the church is the pillar and ground of the truth. It is our responsibility to preserve, promote and proclaim the truth of God in the generation in which we live. Truth is the legacy we have received from the preceding generations of God's saints, and truth is the legacy we must leave to the generations that follow. And that particular body of truth which we are responsible to maintain is the gospel of Christ. Our creed is, and ever must be, 'Jesus Christ and him crucified'. The truth we must preserve and declare is the great 'mystery of godliness', redemption by Jesus Christ, the incarnate God.

We must never lose sight of our purpose. The church of God is not a social welfare agency, though we gladly help the poor and needy. The church is not a counselling centre, though we proclaim to all men all the counsel of God. The church is not an educational centre, though we make known to men the manifold wisdom of God. The church is not a political arena, or even a rallying place for morality, patriotism and the home. It is true, the church of God does influence the political world, the moral, ethical and educational values of society and the stability of the home and family, but our goal, our object, our purpose is the glory of God. Our work is the preaching of the gospel. Our mission is the salvation of God's elect. Our reason for gathering as the house of God is to worship the Lord our God.

The church of God is a preaching centre, a mission station, a sounding board for the gospel of our Lord Jesus Christ. Our single purpose is to proclaim to all men and women the glorious gospel of Christ, the incarnate God, who came into this world to save sinners and has effectually done so for the glory of God. Preaching is our mandate, our strength and our only business in this world. By the support of pastors, missionaries and evangelists who faithfully preach the gospel of Christ, the church of God fulfils her divine commission (Matt. 28:18-20). This is the purpose for our existence in this world.

3. How is the church to be governed?

There is much controversy here. Some say the church must be governed by an ecclesiastical hierarchy, others by a board of elders, others by a board of deacons and others by the democratic vote of the people. Some say that the matter of church government is not plainly revealed in the Word of God. The fact is, none of these forms of church government has any biblical foundation, but the Word of God does tell us plainly how the church is to be governed.

At first the church was under the direct government of Christ himself. Then it was governed by the apostles of our Lord. These apostles appointed deacons to relieve them of the mundane duties of watching over matters of money, property and the care of widows. As the apostles died out the pastors they had appointed in different places had the responsibility of being overseers of the churches. In the New Testament the pastor is sometimes called an 'elder' or a 'bishop'. But wherever you read the words 'elder', 'bishop' or 'pastor' in the New Testament, the men mentioned are men called and gifted of God as the undershepherds of Christ to be the spiritual overseers and rulers of his church.

The church of God is not an organization to be ruled by the democratic vote of the people, or the whims of men. The commonly accepted practice of congregational rule is without foundation, either by precept or precedent, in the Word of God. The church of God is a kingdom under the rule of Christ. It is to be governed by Christ's appointed pastors through the Word of God, as they are led and taught by the Spirit of God (Heb. 13:7, 17).

It is every faithful pastor's responsibility to rule in the house of God (1 Tim. 3:1-7; 1 Peter 5:1-3). He must take the oversight of the church he serves. He does not rule by brute force, intimidation or legislative power, but by the Word of God. His authority is the gospel he preaches. He rules by example, leading the people of God in the way of faith and faithfulness. As God's overseer he rules the church in love, in love for Christ, the truth of God and the people of God. The church of God is not to be ruled by the voice of the people, but by the voice of God through his messenger.

I am aware of the fact that giving one man so much power over so many can be a very dangerous thing, if that man is not himself ruled by the Spirit of Christ. Many have suffered greatly by the abuse of pastoral authority. However, the way to avoid the problem of abuse is not to restrict the pastoral office, but rather to exercise great care in choosing and calling a pastor.

If a congregation really seeks the will of God in calling a pastor rather than their own pleasure, following the leadership of the Holy Spirit rather than their own impressions, and judging a man's gifts, qualifications and abilities by the Word of God rather than by their own standards, they will not need to worry about getting an unfit pastor.

When seeking a pastor the church should get to know everything they possibly can about the man they might want to call, earnestly seek the direction of God the Holy Spirit and carefully follow the guidelines laid down in Holy Scriptures. Once God has given them a faithful pastor, they should earnestly pray for him, seeking God's mercy and grace to abide upon him, preserve him and keep him in the way of truth, faith and righteousness.

When a local church is ruled by the voice of the people, the potential for evil is almost limitless. The Word of God gives four examples of what happens when men and women govern themselves, when the course of action for God's church is determined by the vote of the congregation. The results are a commentary on the subject of congregational rule.

1. In Exodus 32:1-6 the children of Israel are seen dancing naked around the golden calf.
2. In Numbers 16:1-4 the congregation got together, took a vote and decided to kill God's prophet.
3. In 1 Chronicles 13:1-14 David consulted the will of the people and God made a breach upon them, because they defiled the ark of the Lord.
4. In Acts 1:15-26 the church chose an apostle to take Judas' place whom God had not ordained.

The axiom of democracy is 'The people are always right.' But in spiritual matters the people are nearly always wrong. The majority hardly ever rules according to the mind and will of God. Rolfe Barnard used to say, 'If you pray, you don't have to vote. And if you vote, you won't pray.' He was a wise man.

As it is the pastor's responsibility to rule, *it is the responsibility of God's church to follow and obey the man who rules over it as pastor by the will of God.* Again, I emphasize the importance of exercising great care in calling a pastor. Make certain that the man who is called measures up to the requirements that are laid down in Holy Scripture.

The apostle Paul tells us that there are certain things that must be required in the moral and spiritual character of those men who are given the responsibilities of the pastoral office. 'A bishop then must be blameless, the husband of one wife, vigilant, sober, of good behaviour, given to hospitality, apt to teach; not given to wine, no striker, not greedy of filthy lucre; but patient, not a brawler, not covetous; one that ruleth well his own house, having his children in subjection with all gravity; (For if a man know not how to rule his own house, how shall he take care of the church of God?) Not a novice, lest being lifted up with pride he fall into the condemnation of the devil' (1 Tim. 3:2-6). 'A bishop must be blameless, as the steward of God; not self-willed, not soon angry, not given to wine, no striker, not given to filthy lucre; but a lover of hospitality, a lover of good men, sober, just, holy, temperate; holding fast the faithful word as he hath been taught, that he may be able by sound doctrine both to exhort and to convince the gainsayers' (Titus 1:7-9).

If a man does not measure up to these qualifications, no matter how well he seems to preach, no matter how likeable he appears to be, no matter how charming he is, do not call him as pastor. Once a man has been called as pastor, the church has placed herself under his rule. If he is God's man, it will be a blessed relationship. If he is not, it will be a disaster.

It is every believer's responsibility to yield a voluntary subjection and obedience to his pastor, as God's messenger to his soul. 'Remember them which have the rule over you, who have spoken unto you the Word of God: whose faith follow, considering the end of their conversation... Obey them that have the rule over you, and submit yourselves: for they watch for your souls, as they that must give account, that they may do it with joy, and not with grief: for that is unprofitable for you' (Heb. 13:7, 17). This is an obedience based upon love and trust; and it is an obedience which God requires.

If you are not happy with your pastor, if you have reason to question his ability to watch faithfully over your soul, you can do one of two things: either you can ask God to remove him, and quietly wait for him to do so; or you can quietly remove yourself from his rule. In either case you had better be very sure of what you are doing. But do not ever dare to assume that it is your responsibility to remove your pastor! It is God's work alone to unseat pastors in his house. A congregation will be very wise to leave it in God's hands. He says, 'Touch not mine anointed, and do my prophets no harm' (1 Chron. 16:22), and he means it! I have seen many churches remove their pastors from their office. Some appeared to have very justifiable grievances. But I have never seen even one recover from the scars of their action. It is usually devastating. David's noble example should be carefully studied and followed (1 Sam. 26:9-11).

4. How do men and women unite with and join the church of God?

A person is united with the church universal when he is united with Christ by faith. He is born into the church and kingdom of God when he is born again by the Holy Spirit (John 3:3, 5). But a local church must be joined by some public act. I know that some people think that church membership is insignificant; and there are some who place too much importance upon it, making church membership a basis of hope before God. But in the New Testament believers did publicly unite with one another in local churches (Acts 9:26-27; Rom. 16:1-2).

A local church is an assembly, or congregation, of believing men and women united to Christ and one another in love. A local church is a society of saved sinners, knit together by the Spirit of God.

According to the pattern laid down in Acts 2, three things are necessary for membership in the church of God.

1. The person must hear Christ preached (Acts 2:14-40);

2. He or she must believe the gospel and trust the Lord Jesus Christ as he is revealed in the gospel (Acts 2:41);

3. He or she must confess Christ in believer's baptism (Acts 2:41).

Believer's baptism is the door of entrance into the church of God. Baptism does not save anyone. Baptism has no effect upon a man's standing before God; but baptism is the answer of a good conscience towards God (1 Peter 3:21), an act of obedience to Christ (Matt. 28:19) and the believer's public confession of faith in Christ (Rom. 6:4-6). By baptism the believer makes a public identification with and a publicly avowed commitment to Christ, his church and the gospel of his grace.

Every local church, if it is what it should be, if it is truly the church of God, is a habitation of God through the Spirit, the temple of the living God (Eph. 2:20-22; 1 Cor. 3:16). The church is more than a mere unit of men and women. It is a union of hearts. It is more than a bare uniformity of doctrine, though that is essential. It is a union of spiritual life (Eph. 4:1-7). The church is 'one body', united to Christ the Head. All the true members of the church of God live in and by 'one Spirit', the Spirit of Christ. Every member has 'one hope'. Our one hope is Jesus Christ our substitute. We hope for eternal life and acceptance with God only by the righteousness of his life, the atonement of his blood and the power of his intercession. Every member of the church of God owns and submits to 'one Lord', our crucified, risen and exalted Redeemer, Jesus Christ, the Son of God. All God's saints live by 'one faith', the faith of Christ who loved us and gave himself for us. The object of our faith is one — Jesus Christ. The source of our faith is one — the grace of God. The doctrine of our faith is one — the gospel of God's free and sovereign grace in Christ, the sinner's substitute. The goal of our faith is one — the glory of God. Every member of the church has been buried with Christ by 'one baptism' into his death. And all the members worship 'one God', who is the Father of us all. We worship the great, glorious, eternal, sovereign triune Jehovah, Father, Son and Holy Spirit, as he is revealed in the man Christ Jesus.

These are the things which characterize the church of God. If they characterize the church of which you are a part, you have the blessed privilege of being in the church of God. If they do not, your church is nothing but a religious club, which has a name that it lives, but is dead!

5. What does church membership involve?

It is one thing to have your name on a church roll, but something else altogether to be a member of the church of God. Church membership is an alliance of hearts to one another in Christ. It is a voluntary commitment of love, a loving commitment to Christ and to one another for Christ's sake. To unite with the church of God is to make a public commitment to the worship of Christ, the gospel of Christ and the church of Christ.

1. *We are committed to the worship of our Lord Jesus Christ.* We come together to read his Word, sing his praises, observe his ordinances, seek his grace, call upon his name and be instructed in the doctrine of his gospel (Acts 2:42).

2. *We are committed to the gospel of Christ.* God's church is united in the defence of the gospel and committed to the furtherance of the gospel. For this reason the saints meet together as often as they can to hear the Word, give as much as they can to publish the Word and go forth to proclaim the Word. Together God's people give of their means to support one man and his family, so that he can give himself to the ministry of the Word, in prayer and study, so that when he stands to preach, he will be able to feed them with knowledge and understanding (Jer. 3:15). Together the local assembly of God's saints give of their means to support faithful missionaries, evangelists and pastors of smaller, poorer churches around the world, so that they may publish the gospel around the world without the distraction of earthly cares. And, together, local congregations give of their means to pay for and distribute gospel tracts, tapes and books around the world, to purchase airtime on radio and television, so that men and women everywhere may hear the gospel and live. Why? Because the church of God is committed to the gospel of Christ!

3. *We are committed to the church of Christ.* God's saints are committed to one another for Christ's sake. Find an assembly of men and women, anywhere in the world, which is the church of God, and

you will find an assembly of people whose hearts are devoted to one
another in love (Phil. 2:1-4). God's people love each other! They
pray for one another. They help one another. They encourage one
another. They comfort one another. They forgive one another.

6. Why should you unite with the church of God?

Perhaps some of my readers are at this very time debating the matter
of church membership in their own hearts. They may be looking for
biblical reasons to unite publicly with the church of God. I could
give such a person numerous reasons from the Scriptures why he or
she should unite with a local New Testament church. But I will give
you just one: if you are a believer, if you trust the Lord Jesus Christ,
if you are born again by the grace and power of God's Holy Spirit,
you should unite with the church of God because *you need them.*
You need the regular ministry of the gospel, that you may grow in
the grace and knowledge of Christ. You need the fellowship of
God's family, and you need the comfort, help, strength and encouragement of God's children (Heb. 10:24-25).

The church of God is neither more nor less than an assembly of
men and women whose hearts are united together in the faith of the
gospel, the fellowship of the Spirit and the love of Jesus Christ.
Against this church the gates of hell can never prevail (Matt. 16:18).
To this church the Lord Jesus Christ has promised perfect, complete,
everlasting glory (Eph. 5:25-27).

3.
The necessity for faithful pastors

'Take heed therefore unto yourselves, and to all the flock, over the which the Holy Ghost hath made you overseers, to feed the church of God, which he hath purchased with his own blood. For I know this, that after my departing shall grievous wolves enter in among you, not sparing the flock. Also of your own selves shall men arise, speaking perverse things, to draw away disciples after them. Therefore watch, and remember, that by the space of three years I ceased not to warn everyone night and day with tears. And now, brethren, I commend you to God, and to the word of his grace, which is able to build you up, and to give you an inheritance among all them which are sanctified' (Acts 20:28-32).

In Jeremiah 3:15 God promised his church, 'I will give you pastors according to mine heart, which shall feed you with knowledge and understanding.' In that promise, three things are clearly stated.

1. *True pastors are the gifts of God's own heart to his church.*
Indeed, the greatest blessing God can ever bestow upon any local church in this world is to give that church a faithful pastor, a man who preaches the gospel of his free and sovereign grace in Christ (Isa. 52:7; Rom. 10:15).

2. *Faithful, God-given pastors, pastors according to God's own heart, are men who feed the flock of God.* They do not fleece the

sheep, beat the sheep, use the sheep, or abuse the sheep. They feed the sheep! Their life work is the business of feeding the people of God, and they give themselves to their work ardently.

3. *Those men whom God gives to his church as pastors feed the church of God with knowledge and understanding.* Those who are called of God to feed his people have a God-given knowledge of divine truth and a God-given understanding of the needs of his people in this world, and they feed them accordingly.

In these dark days the church of God has suffered much abuse at the hands of unfaithful, self-seeking, self-serving pastors, who make merchandise of men's souls and handle the Word of God deceitfully. But God promised to give his church pastors who would be faithful to their souls, and he does what he promised. When our Lord Jesus Christ ascended up into heaven as the Head of his church, one of his ascension gifts to the church was 'pastors and teachers, for the perfecting of the saints, for the work of the ministry, for the edifying of the body of Christ' (Eph. 4:11-12). These men are the angels of God to his churches (Rev. 1:16-20). They are heaven-sent messengers of grace and truth.

The one thing the church must have in this world is faithful pastors. She cannot get along without faithful men, called, gifted and ordained of God for the work of the ministry. We do not have to have fine buildings in which to meet. We can meet in barns, or in the woods, if we must, but the church of God cannot survive in this world without faithful pastors, men committed to the gospel and gifted of God to preach it.

In the course of a year, I preach to a good number of congregations in the United States and in other countries. Some are just getting started; some have been around for a long time. But, for some reason, many of these churches have no pastor. God has not yet given them a man to speak to their hearts in his name. I am always anxious to do what I can to help these churches, and there is one thing I always try to impress upon them: the first priority of every local church must be to get a pastor, get him well established and make whatever sacrifices are required to do so. That is the first order of business for a local church. And to all who may read these pages, I say, without qualification, if God is not pleased to send a faithful pastor to you, you will be wise to sell out and move to a place where there is a man faithfully preaching the gospel of his free grace in Christ.

A church without a pastor is like a body without a head: dead, useless and decaying! Sheep must have a shepherd. They cannot survive long without one. It is not possible to over-emphasize the necessity for faithful pastors to the church of God.

The apostle Paul knew the dangers he faced as a gospel preacher, and he knew the dangers God's church would have to face in this world for the gospel's sake. Therefore, when he called the elders of the church at Ephesus together for his last meeting with them, he gave them a most solemn charge. Luke records the event and Paul's message to those Ephesian elders in Acts 20. In the first part of his message (vv. 17-27), Paul told them how he had behaved as God's servant among them, 'serving the Lord with all humility of mind', and preaching the gospel of Christ. In public and in private, for three years, Paul had preached the gospel to the Ephesians. He had declared to them 'all the counsel of God'. So plainly and faithfully had he preached the gospel to them that he called his hearers to be his witnesses and declared, 'I take you to record this day, that I am pure from the blood of all men.' Then, in verses 28-32, Paul addressed himself to the elders who would be left behind to carry on the work of the gospel after him. In these verses he shows us both the responsibility of, and the necessity for, faithful pastors. Using Paul's message to the Ephesian elders, I want to raise and answer three basic questions about the work of the gospel ministry.

1. What is the pastor's responsibility?

Most people think that a pastor's work is mostly that of a social worker, promoter and psychoanalyst. They see the work of a pastor in terms of hospital visiting, taking tea with old ladies, playing with children, involvement in community affairs, getting people to join the church, conducting weddings and funerals and counselling those with problems. But the Word of God never mentions any of these things in describing pastoral work.

It is every pastor's responsibility to do the work of an evangelist, seeking the salvation of God's elect and helping to establish local churches (2 Tim. 4:5). The sphere of a pastor's ministry is limited

only by the providence of God. Every man who is gifted for the work
of the ministry has a responsibility to preach the gospel to all men
in his generation, in so far as God permits him to do so, exercising
his gifts in the widest range possible for the glory of Christ. Every
open door must be entered and every opportunity must be seized for
the furtherance of the gospel. The local church has no right to place
any restrictions upon the pastor's ministry, and a faithful man will
not allow himself to be hindered in the preaching of the gospel.

Yet the principal sphere of a pastor's ministry is the local church
over which the Lord has placed him. He must not allow his
responsibilities to minister to his own assembly to be neglected. We
must not neglect the lost, or the needs of God's church at large, but
the primary concern of every faithful pastor is the congregation of
believers which God has entrusted to his care. In Acts 20:28 the
apostle Paul shows us five things about the pastor's responsibility.

1. *The pastor must take heed unto himself.* Paul's words to every
pastor of every age are, 'Take heed unto yourselves.' That simply
means, 'Pastor, be sure you do not neglect your own soul. Ever be
mindful of your relationship with God and of your responsibilities
as the servant of God (1 Tim. 4:16). Let nothing sidetrack you,
interfere with your studies, your preaching of the gospel and prayer,
and let nothing turn your heart away from Christ.'

The most constant danger God's servant faces in this world is the
neglect of his own soul, while endeavouring to minister to the souls
of others. Therefore Paul says, 'Take heed unto yourselves.' Let
every pastor take heed to the gifts God has given him, to use them
and improve them, and be careful not to neglect them. The pastor
must take heed to his time, spending it wisely in prayer, in study, in
preaching, not squandering it away. He must take heed to his own
heart, his own spirit and his own life. He must ever be watchful over
the motives of his heart, make certain that his spirit is not ruled by
passion and see to it that his life exemplifies the gospel he preaches.
He must also constantly take heed to his doctrine, making certain
that his doctrine is the pure doctrine of Christ, the doctrine of the
gospel, the doctrine of pure, free, sovereign, eternal, effectual grace
in the Lord Jesus Christ, the sinner's substitute. To these things
every pastor must constantly and carefully give his undivided
attention (1 Tim. 4:12-16). The man who neglects these things is not
fit for the pastoral office.

2. *The pastor is a shepherd who must take care of and tend to all the flock of God.* He must take heed to himself 'and unto all the flock'. The church of God is compared to a flock of sheep which is tended and watched over by faithful shepherds, gospel preachers. The word 'pastor' simply means 'shepherd'. Christ Jesus is the Chief Shepherd to whom the flock belongs. Pastors are his appointed under-shepherds, whose responsibility it is to take care of the flock (1 Peter 5:1-4).

Remember the Lord's people in this world, are, like their pastors (cf. John 21:15-17), fickle, sinful, helpless, defenceless, stumbling, falling sheep. Because they are sheep they need shepherds, pastors, to care lovingly for them.

It is the pastor's responsibility to watch over the flock which the Chief Shepherd has committed to his care. He must watch over and care for 'all the flock', the weak and the strong, the immature and the mature, the foolish and the wise, the old and the young, the fallen and the stable. He must watch over all the flock at all times and in all circumstances. It is the pastor's responsibility to feed the sheep with knowledge and understanding, protect the sheep with his very life, lead the sheep by going before them, encourage and comfort the sheep with the gospel, help the sheep in trouble and sometimes gently carry the sheep in loving arms; but it is never his responsibility to chasten the sheep. The Chief Shepherd alone has the wisdom and ability to do that!

3. *It is every pastor's responsibility to be an overseer over the church of God.* Let us notice carefully the language Paul uses: 'Take heed therefore unto yourselves, and to all the flock, over the which the Holy Ghost hath made you overseers.' It is true, the pastor is himself one of the sheep, and he must not be a dictator, lording it over God's heritage, imposing his will upon the church. The church belongs to Christ, not to the pastor. But every man who is called of God to the work of the gospel ministry is responsible under God to take the oversight of the church of God which he serves (1 Peter 5:1-3). The care of the church is his responsibility. The pastor is responsible to rule the church of God in exactly the same way as a husband is responsible to rule over his own house (1 Tim. 3:4-5).

The pastor must rule by example, not by intimidation; by love, not by legislation; by the Word of God, not his own word; according to the will of God, not according to his own will. He must win the respect of men and women, so that they are willing to be ruled by him, but rule he must! His faith and faithfulness are to be followed, and his rule is to be obeyed (Heb. 13:7,17). Someone has to be in charge, and the person ordained of God to take charge of his church is the man he places as pastor over his church. God does not trifle with those who refuse to submit to and obey his messengers (Num. 16:1-35).

4. *It is the pastor's primary responsibility to feed the church of God.* Everything else in this verse of Scripture might almost be read as a parenthesis. This was Paul's message to the Ephesian elders and to every pastor today: 'Take heed unto yourselves... to feed the church of God.' It is the pastor's responsibility to feed the church with knowledge and understanding, with knowledge of pure gospel doctrine and understanding of the peculiar needs of his hearers. Such knowledge and understanding can be obtained only by diligent study and prayer. It is the responsibility of the church to see to it that its pastor's needs are fully met, so that he may give himself to study and prayer, not having to worry about the earthly, material needs of his family. And it is the pastor's responsibility to spend his life in study, prayer and preaching. If he does, he will have that God-given knowledge and understanding required to minister to the hearts of God's elect. If he does not give himself relentlessly to the study of Holy Scripture and prayer, he is not fit to be a pastor, for he has no food for the sheep. The sooner he stops pretending to be a pastor the better.

Fancy oratory may tickle the brain and tear-jerking stories may stir the emotions; but only plain gospel doctrine will inform the mind, convict the conscience, subdue the will and win the heart. The church of God can never be strong if it is ignorant. It can never accomplish anything of value if it is uninformed. All preachers called of God are doctrinal preachers, men who instruct God's saints in divine truth. The preacher without doctrine is like a shotgun without a load: empty, full of air and useless!

Gospel preachers are preachers of doctrine, and the doctrine we must preach is Jesus Christ and him crucified. The doctrine of the Bible is the doctrine of the cross. The doctrine of the cross is the revelation of God's glory in redemption, the hope of helpless sinners, the motive for all obedience, the strength against all temptation, the comfort in every trial, the rule by which we live and the gate through which we enter into the kingdom of God. Christ crucified is milk for babies, meat for men, ointment for the aged, fire for the cold, balm for the wounded, armour for the warrior, strength for the weak, help for the tempted, hope for the fallen and joy for all the redeemed.

5. *The work of the gospel ministry is an awesome burden of responsibility,* because the church which the pastor serves is 'the church of God, which he hath purchased with his own blood'. The price of our purchase was the precious blood of Christ (1 Peter 1:18-19). The church, the multitude of God's elect, like all other men, by nature were born under the sentence of death, fallen, depraved and guilty (Eph. 2:4), deserving of eternal ruin. Only the blood of Christ could remove the curse from us and deliver us from the hands of divine justice. And Christ, by his own life-blood, has effectually accomplished the redemption of his people (Gal. 3:13; Heb. 9:12).

The transaction which took place at Calvary between God the Father, God the Son and God the Spirit was a legal purchase. Jesus Christ paid the price of our ransom to the offended justice of God (1 Peter 3:18). Justice, being satisfied, has no claim upon those for whom Christ died, his elect bride, the church (Rom. 8:1). Having paid the price of our redemption, the Son of God obtained his purchased possession.

We belong to Jesus twice:
He has bought us with a price.
He is our Creator God,
And he bought us with his blood.

Notice the distinguishing character of God's sovereign grace. The Lord Jesus Christ has done for his church what he does for no one else (Eph. 5:25-27). Christ loved his church with an everlasting love, as it was chosen for and given to him by God the Father before the world began. Christ purchased his church with a particular and effectual blood redemption. The Lord Jesus cleanses his church by the grace and power of his Holy Spirit in regeneration. He nourishes his church and cherishes it, ever preserving it by his grace, and he will present his church in the perfection of beauty and holiness in ultimate glorification.

The church of God, so precious to the triune God, is committed to the care of faithful pastors. Let none abuse it, but serve it with ardent love and diligent faithfulness.

2. Why are pastors necessary?

All of God's saints are kings and priests unto God through Christ Jesus. We need no earthly priests, mediators, or intercessors. God the Holy Spirit teaches all his elect. Every believer has an unction from God and knows the truth. Why, then, is it necessary for the church to have pastors? Here are three answers to that question given in the Word of God.

1. *Pastors are necessary because this is the purpose of God for his church* (Jer. 3:15). God has ordained the salvation of his elect by the means of gospel preaching (1 Cor. 1:21-23; Rom. 10:9-17; James 1:18). The only way God speaks to men is through men, in the faithful exposition of Holy Scripture (Acts 8:31). God does speak directly to the hearts of his people by his Spirit through the Word, but that personal understanding, given in private study and worship, comes as the result of and in conjunction with the public ministry of the Word, never apart from it. Sheep must be guided and fed by a shepherd. The Lord would not have given pastors to be teachers in his kingdom if they were not needed. God never gives what his people do not need.

Beware of any doctrine you learn on your own. It is a common saying among men, 'The man who is his own lawyer has a fool for a lawyer.' And I assure you that the person who is his own prophet has a fool for a prophet. God teaches men and women his Word, his will and his truth by faithful gospel preachers.

2. *God has given pastors to his church for the edification of the body of Christ* (Eph. 4:12-16). The word 'edify' simply means 'to build up'. Once God's elect are converted by the preaching of the gospel, they are built up in the faith by that same gospel preaching. It is by the preaching of the gospel that men and women learn the truth, and it is by the preaching of the gospel that they learn to apply the truth of God to their lives and walk in it.

3. *The Lord has given his church pastors according to his own heart for the protection of his people from the influence of error and heresy* (Eph. 4:14; 2 Tim. 3:1-4:5; Acts 20:29-31). Pastors must ever keep watch over the flock, like diligent shepherds, lest grievous wolves enter in with their pernicious doctrines and by their cunning subtlety destroy it. The pastor must expose the wolves, sometimes calling them by name, as Paul did in 2 Timothy. If he would be faithful to the souls of men, the gospel of Christ and the glory of God, the pastor must expose every doctrine that is contrary to the gospel of God's free and sovereign grace in Christ. He must nip it in the bud as soon as it appears. He must constantly, fervently and compassionately warn the people of God, expose every error of free will, legalism, liberalism and works religion. He must labour to build up the house of God upon the sure foundation of the gospel, the substitutionary atonement of Christ and the free grace of God in him.

3. What is the security of the church against every onslaught of heresy?

The only sure protection that God's church has from the heresies that abound in this world is the Word of God. This was Paul's final word to his brethren at Ephesus: 'And now, brethren, I commend you to God, and to the word of his grace, which is able to build you up, and to give you an inheritance among all them which are sanctified' (Acts 20:32).

The pastor must faithfully feed the church of God with sound gospel doctrine, endeavour to expose every grievous wolf who would turn them away from simple faith in Christ and expound the gospel of God's free and sovereign grace in Christ to all who hear him. Let every pastor constantly hold before his hearers the wonders of redemption and the glory of grace. But the security of the church is God himself (Matt. 16:18). Child of God, ever trust Christ and adhere tenaciously to the word of his grace (2 Tim. 1:13). The gospel of Christ will make you strong, and the gospel of Christ will bring you to glory.

If you have read this far, I can reasonably assume that it is your genuine interest in the cause of Christ that has led you to do so. Therefore I conclude this chapter with the hope that it has helped you to see more clearly the necessity for faithful pastors. I commend to you two quotations from the apostle Paul, without comment, for your personal meditation.

'We beseech you, brethren, to know them which labour among you, and are over you in the Lord, and admonish you; and to esteem them very highly in love for their work's sake. And be at peace among yourselves' (1 Thess. 5:12-13).

'Finally, brethren, pray for us, that the word of the Lord may have free course, and be glorified, even as it is with you' (2 Thess. 3:1).

4.
The character and conduct of faithful pastors

'This is a true saying, If a man desire the office of a bishop, he desireth a good work. A bishop then must be blameless, the husband of one wife, vigilant, sober, of good behaviour, given to hospitality, apt to teach; not given to wine, no striker, not greedy of filthy lucre; but patient, not a brawler, not covetous; one that ruleth well his own house, having his children in subjection with all gravity; (for if a man know not how to rule his own house, how shall he take care of the church of God?) not a novice, lest being lifted up with pride he fall into the condemnation of the devil. Moreover, he must have a good report of them which are without; lest he fall into reproach and the snare of the devil' (1 Tim. 3:1-7).

'For a bishop must be blameless, as the steward of God; not self-willed, not soon angry, not given to wine, no striker, not given to filthy lucre; but a lover of hospitality, a lover of good men, sober, just, holy, temperate; holding fast the faithful word as he hath been taught, that he may be able by sound doctrine both to exhort and convince the gainsayers' (Titus 1:7-9).

In these two portions of Holy Scripture the apostle Paul tells us precisely what kind of man a pastor must be. By the infallible inspiration of God the Holy Spirit the church of God is given a list of plain, unmistakable gifts and qualities it must require of any man who is called and ordained to preach the gospel. Sooner or later, every local church will be faced with the responsibility of calling a man to fill its pulpit and rule over it as the messenger of God.

Whether the church's pulpit committee is a board of elders, a board of deacons, or a group of men specifically appointed to find a man to fill the pulpit, the first, most important responsibility of that pulpit committee is to make certain that the man they recommend to the church meets every criterion required in these two passages of Scripture.

The importance of this responsibility cannot be over-emphasized. The church must get to know everything it can about a man before he is called as pastor. It must determine whether the man to be called meets the qualifications of character and conduct given by the Holy Spirit. If the church does not find out what kind of man a preacher is until after he has been called as pastor, it will be too late to do much about it then. Much of the trouble churches have is the result of carelessness in calling a pastor, or of downright disregard for the instructions given in the Word of God. It does not matter how well a man can preach, how orthodox he is, how warm, friendly and charming he is, or how handsome he is, if a man does not meet the requirements of 1 Timothy 3:1-7 and Titus 1:7-9, he must not be given the honour and responsibility of ruling the house of God as pastor.

The pastor must be a man of exemplary character and conduct, whose faithfulness sets the pattern by which others are to live for the glory of Christ and the furtherance of the gospel (1 Tim. 4:12). Any man whose personal character and conduct does not exemplify the gospel of Christ has no business preaching the gospel in any pulpit. The preacher whose life is contrary to the gospel of the grace of God mocks his hearers, brings reproach upon the gospel and dishonours the name of the Lord Jesus Christ. Those who do not, by their lives, exemplify gospel principles have no business instructing others in the gospel, or leading others in the worship of God.

I have said that a church should find out everything it can about a man before calling him as pastor. Let me re-emphasize that point and offer some advice. When a church is seeking a pastor it would be very wise to solicit the recommendations of credible, experienced, faithful men. Try to find out what reputation a man has, what his employment record is, what his credit record is, what kind of family he has, how his children behave, whether he is dependable, faithful and respected in the church of which he is a member, and what kind of relationship he has with those who know him best. These things will tell much about a man's spiritual character, and these things must be considered before a man is called as pastor of a congregation. Once he is seated and established as pastor, it is too late. A church which tries to get rid of a pastor who is less than desirable is much like a woman divorcing a man who turns out not to be what she expected — it is a painful mess, hurting many people, and leaves scars from which recovery is very unlikely.

I highly recommend any church to go to the trouble and expense of having a prospective preacher bring his entire family to stay in the area for a week or two, before he is called, just to get acquainted. It would be money well spent.

To be God's messenger to, and pastor of, a congregation of God's saints in this world, however small, is the highest, most noble, most honourable, most responsible, most demanding office, position and work in the world. That church is an assembly of men and women who are loved of God, redeemed by the blood of Christ and called by the Holy Spirit. Such a remarkable office demands men of remarkable character. This remarkable character is in no way a matter of natural excellence, ability, or superiority. It is altogether the work of God's grace. You can be sure of this: if God calls a man to the work of the gospel ministry, God will see to it that that man possesses the qualifications required in his Word for the pastoral office. Basically, the qualifications required of any man who is given the privilege and responsibility of the pastoral office are fourfold.

1. The pastor must be a man who has experienced, who believes and who preaches the gospel of the grace of God (Titus 1:9; 2 Tim. 1:9-13; Eph. 3:7-12)

A man cannot tell what he does not know any more than he can come back from where he has not been. And no man can preach the gospel with the power of God, to the good of men's hearts and souls, until he has experienced the gospel. No greater curse could ever fall upon a congregation of men and women in this world than for them to have a graceless, spiritually dead man in the pulpit.

The pastor must be a man who is born again by the almighty grace of God. I am often asked, 'Why would any man want to be a preacher if he is not born again?' There are many answers to that question, but it is enough simply to recognize that there always have been, and are today, many preachers who are yet dead in trespasses and sins. Judas, Simon Magus, Demas, Diotrephes, Hymenæus and Philetus all had three things in common: all were preachers; all were lost, and all lost their own souls in hell! Without question, those preachers who do not know and preach the gospel of God's free grace in Christ are lost, but it is also possible for a man to be precisely accurate in doctrine and yet not to know Christ. The first matter of importance is that the man called to be pastor of the church of God must be born again.

The pastor must be a man. The ordination of women is clearly contrary to the teaching of the Word of God. Women are to be silent in the church (1 Cor. 14:34). If they are silent, they cannot very well preach. Women are to be in subjection, never usurping authority over men (1 Tim. 2:11-12). If they are not to be in authority over men, women cannot be allowed to rule the house of God. Only those who reject the authority of God's Word and set aside his clear commands would consider the ordination of women to office in the church.

No man should be called and ordained as the pastor of any church who does not firmly believe and consistently preach the gospel of God's free and sovereign grace in Christ. Let me be perfectly plain and clear. No man has any business preaching who is not committed to the preaching of the gospel. His preaching must be thoroughly and unmistakably Calvinistic. There is no room for an Arminian, or a teacher of free will, in the pulpit of God's church. It is not enough that the preacher simply gives lip-service to the doctrines of grace. Divine sovereignty, total depravity, unconditional election, limited atonement, irresistible grace and the sure perseverance of God's elect must be the steady, uncompromising message of every man who is allowed to speak in God's name to men and women who are facing the prospect of eternity. We cannot, and would not if we could, control the speech of godless men, but in the church of God the errors of free-will, works, man-centred religion cannot be tolerated. The church must demand of her pastors total commitment to the preaching of the gospel of grace alone, Christ alone, faith alone. There is no middle ground.

The man given the honour of the pastoral office must be a man whose preaching is Christ-centred. That is to say, he must preach Christ crucified as the essence, foundation and fulness of all truth, the motive for all obedience, the inspiration for all worship, the pattern for all godliness and the theme of all Scripture. Christ is all in the book of God (Luke 24:27, 44-47). Christ is all in the work of salvation (1 Cor. 1:30). Christ is all in the church of God (Col. 3:11). Christ is all in the purpose of God (Rom. 8:29). And Christ is all in the preaching of all preachers called by God (1 Cor. 2:2).

In a word, *the man who serves as pastor over God's church is to be a man whose preaching is spiritual.* His doctrine must be accurate, precisely orthodox, but that alone is not enough. His preaching must be spiritual. He must, if he would be useful, come directly to the pulpit from the throne of God with a fresh message from God's heart burning in his own heart to deliver to the hearts of God's elect. Only by the Spirit of God is it possible for a man to do so.

2. The pastor must be a man of mature spiritual character

He must be a man whose life exemplifies the gospel of Christ. No man can be given the charge of the church who is not of mature spiritual character.

He must not be a novice (1 Tim. 3:6). The word 'novice' does not mean 'one who is young'. Timothy was a young man (1 Tim. 4:12), but he was not a novice. A novice is 'one newly come into the faith', or 'one newly planted'. A novice is a young, inexperienced convert, one who is untried and unproven. Such a man must never be given the responsibility of pastoring a church, 'lest being lifted up with pride he fall into condemnation of the devil'.

The gospel preacher must also be a man of competent knowledge and understanding in the Scriptures. It is the responsibility of a pastor to feed the church of God with knowledge and understanding (Jer. 3:15; Acts 20:28). Without question, that includes many things beyond doctrinal instruction, but it certainly includes doctrinal instruction. No man can feed others with knowledge of the things of God if he lacks that knowledge himself.

The pastor must have a God-given ability to comprehend and teach the Scriptures (2 Tim. 2:1-2). This competent, spiritual understanding of the Word of God is not the result of good training, or even diligent study, though that is necessary. It is the gift of Christ himself (Eph. 4:7-8, 11-16; Gal. 1:11-12). It is a heart-knowledge of the gospel. But knowledge alone is not enough.

The pastor must be apt to teach (1 Tim. 3:2). He must be well-versed in Holy Scripture, so that he rightly discerns the truth of God (2 Tim. 2:15), but he must also possess the God-given ability to preach the gospel to others. He must be able to proclaim the most sublime, glorious mysteries of the gospel with childlike simplicity. Is it any wonder that Paul asked the Ephesians to pray for him, that utterance might be given to him? (Eph. 6:19).

The gospel preacher is not called to explain meticulous points of theology, or debate meaningless questions. He is called of God to proclaim divine truth in unmistakable terms, to set forth Jesus Christ crucified before perishing sinners, to call upon those same perishing sinners to look to the Lamb of God and be saved and to persuade them to do so immediately.

The man into whose hands such a mighty weight of responsibility is given must be a man of proven faithfulness, dependability, commitment and service to the church of Christ. The best training ground for a gospel preacher is not a Bible college, or seminary, but a local church. I recommend to any man who 'desires the office of a pastor' that he find his place in a gospel church, under the ministry of a proven, faithful pastor, and commit himself to the service of Christ in that church in any capacity, submitting to and learning everything he can from that pastor. Any man who is not a dependable, faithful, committed church member, of proven value and service to the church of Christ, would be a worthless minister. Such a man ought never to be placed in a pulpit. The language of the Bible is unmistakable — 'not a novice'!

3. The pastor must be a man of manly, responsible domestic character (1 Tim. 3:4-5)

As we have seen, it is a pastor's responsibility to rule the church of God, as God's representative and spokesman. He does not rule by intimidation and brute force, but by a loving example of commitment, faithfulness and unbending dedication to the glory of God. But he does rule. He cannot be a timid, cowardly weakling, who can be intimidated, overrun and forced into compromise. A man's domestic life will reveal whether he is manly or weak, responsible or irresponsible.

He must be the husband of one wife (1 Tim. 3:2). This does not mean that a pastor must be a married man. (All that I have seen and learned in my experience as a pastor tells me that it is unwise for a man to pastor a church who is not married. I do not recommend it. But the Word of God does not require that a man be married.) Nor does Paul mean that a man who has been married more than once cannot be a pastor. This is simply an injunction against allowing a polygamist to be pastor of a church. In the early Gentile churches, and in some societies today, this was a very needful injunction. If a polygamist was converted, he was not required to abandon his wives and children, but he was not allowed to pastor a church, lest it appear that the gospel of Christ condones such wickedness. Literally, the words, 'the husband of one wife', mean 'a man who has but one wife' or, as John Gill says, 'that he should have but one wife at a time'.

The pastor must be a man who exercises headship, authority and rule over his household. This requirement is unpopular today, but it is still God's order of things. Every man is responsible under God to rule his own house for the glory of God, and any man who does not do so is not fit for the gospel ministry. Joshua did not say, 'I want to serve the Lord, but my wife and children have decided not to do so.' He said, 'As for me and my house, we will serve the Lord' (Josh. 14:15). And they did!

There is no room in the ministry for weak, hen-pecked men with domineering wives, or for men who have no control of their children, men who neglect and despise their God-given responsibilities. If a man does not have the respect of his wife and children, if they do not give him the respect required to rule his house, he is not man enough to gain the respect and reverence required to rule a congregation.

4. The pastor must be a man of exemplary personal character (1 Tim. 3:2-3, 7; Titus 1:7-8)

Above all other things the matter of personal character and conduct is neglected by churches when they consider calling a pastor. Yet it is the preacher's weaknesses of character and unbecoming conduct which are most quickly spotted by the world and the church. Surely, it would be wise for a congregation to find out all it can about a man's personal character before calling him to be its pastor. This is a matter of great importance, not to be taken lightly. It matters not how sound a man is in doctrine, or how gifted he is in preaching, or how submissive his wife and children are; if his personal life is contrary to the gospel of Christ, he must not be given the responsibility of pastoring a church.

The pastor must be a man of blameless behaviour. I do not mean that he is to be blameless in the eyes of God, or that he is to live in sinless perfection. No man is blameless before God, or without sin, except by the substitutionary work of Christ. By his blood atonement and imputed righteousness all believers are 'holy and without blame before him' (Eph. 1:4), but no man lives without sin. Paul's meaning is that the pastor must be a man who lives above the reproach of the world, so that none can justly charge him with indecency, dishonesty, or lack of principle and integrity.

Two things will ruin a man's ministry and destroy the church he pastors quicker and more surely than anything else. These two things are sexual immorality and bad debts. Seldom, if ever, does the man or the church recover from those two things. The church should be willing to forgive any failure, but the tenor of a man's life, his character, tells what he is. If the characteristics of his life are evil, it is likely that the man is evil.

The pastor must be a man of good report. That simply means that he is to be a man whose reputation is consistent with the gospel of the grace of God. To those within the church he must be an example in word, in faith, in charity, in spirit, in faithfulness and in purity (1 Tim. 4:12). In all things the pastor must lead the way, not in word only, but in practice, by personal example. In his epistles the apostle Paul spoke to men and women four times saying, 'Be ye followers of me' (1 Cor. 4:16; 11:1; Phil. 3:17; 1 Thess. 1:6). It is customary for men to say to their children, 'Do as I say, not as I do.' But a pastor must so live before men that he can say to the people of God, 'Do as I do.'

Before the world without the pastor must so live that he has a good report, even among those who have no interest in the gospel. No one can stop wicked men from slanderous gossip and scandalous accusations. Our Lord Jesus was accused of being a glutton, a winebibber and a devilish man, and every faithful preacher since Christ Jesus has had to endure having his name and reputation dragged through the mud of scandalous rumour and gossip. But those who preach the gospel must so live that no man can justly charge them of being men of questionable character and conduct. God's servants must live blamelessly, so that even their enemies know they are men of principle and integrity. The ministry must not be blamed. The way of righteousness must not be mocked. The gospel of the grace of God must not be held in contempt because those who preach it live contemptibly. The name of Christ must not be dishonoured.

The pastor must not be a man given to any vice. He must not be given to wine, that is, to excessive drinking. It is not drinking a glass of wine that is forbidden. That is no more evil than drinking a glass of water. Our Lord turned water to wine (John 2:1-11). It is drunkenness that is forbidden.

He must not be a quarrelsome, contentious, hot-tempered man, but patient and longsuffering.

He must not be a greedy, covetous man. He must not be desirous of, or seek after, wealth, luxury and extravagance. The pastor must be a man of modesty. His life, his family, his style of dress, his car, his home, everything about him must reflect modesty, never luxury and extravagance. How can a man ask others to make sacrifices for the cause of Christ, while he lives in luxury? How can he point men to heaven, while he keeps his hands full of the world?

The pastor must also be given to hospitality, open-hearted, open-handed, generous. Everything he has must evidently belong to Christ and evidently be used for the church of God and the cause of Christ — his home, his table, his car, his money, everything!

To sum it all up, Paul tells us that *a pastor must be a man of vigilance and sobriety* (1 Tim. 3:2). The preacher of the gospel must be a sober-minded, thoughtful man, a man of seriousness and diligence, constantly taking heed to matters of importance. He must seriously keep watch over his own soul. He must diligently give himself to the study of the Word and the labour of the gospel. He must give himself wholly to the ministry of Christ, the preaching of the gospel, and he must constantly maintain a shepherd's careful watch over the church of God.

It is the responsibility of every pastor to give himself faithfully and entirely to the work of the ministry for the glory of Christ, the good of God's church and the salvation of God's elect (2 Tim. 4:1-5; 1 Tim. 4:12-16). Every local church may reasonably expect these things from its pastor.

In return for his labour, and for the success of the gospel, every pastor who faithfully preaches the gospel may reasonably expect the church he serves to meet his and his family's needs, relieving him of every material concern in this world (Gal. 6:6). He deserves the full support and co-operation of those for whom he labours, and he should have both their highest esteem and an interest in their prayers (1Thess. 5:12-13; 2 Thess. 3:1). God will bless the labours of such a man and such a church for the glory of Christ.

5.
The test of a watchman

'So thou, O son of man, I have set thee a watchman unto the house of Israel; therefore thou shalt hear the word at my mouth, and warn them from me. When I say unto the wicked, O wicked man, thou shalt surely die; if thou dost not speak to warn the wicked from his way, that wicked man shall die in his iniquity; but his blood will I require at thine hand. Nevertheless, if thou warn the wicked of his way to turn from it; if he do not turn from his way, he shall die in his iniquity; but thou hast delivered thy soul' (Ezek. 33:7-9).

The old prophets used to speak of 'the burden of the word of the Lord' (Mal. 1:1). They spoke to men and women in deadly earnestness, with fear and trembling. There was no frivolity about them. They were not showmen, but spokesmen. They were not promoters, but prophets. They were sent of God with a message that must be delivered, and they knew the weight of their responsibility.

Preachers today could use some of that prophetic burden. Every preacher, as he enters the pulpit to preach the gospel for the glory of God and the good of men's souls, should have four awesome facts upon his heart.

1. *He is a watchman over the souls of those who hear him.* By divine providence he has been placed upon the walls of Zion, in the particular place of God's appointment, to keep watch over the souls of men. By profession, he claims to be a watchman, one whom God

has set to watch over people in danger, to warn them and show them the way of safety and life.

2. *As a watchman, it is the pastor's responsibility to preach in God's stead to men and women facing eternity* (2 Cor. 5:20). God's servants are God's ambassadors to fallen, depraved, lost men and women. They must hear the word at God's mouth and deliver it, exactly as God gives it, to men and women with undying, immortal souls! It is the responsibility of every preacher, every time he preaches, to make certain that the message he delivers is God's message.

3. *If the pastor is God's messenger, if he delivers God's message, then what he preaches is of eternal consequence* (2 Cor. 2:15-17). If a pastor faithfully delivers God's message in the power of God's Spirit, his message will either save or damn. It will either be a message of life or a message of death to those who hear him. God's servants do not labour in vain. God's Word will never return to him void (Isa. 55:11).

4. *There is a day coming when every watchman will meet every person to whom he has preached, face to face, before the judgement bar of Almighty God to give account of his work* (Heb. 13:17). In that great and terrible day of the Lord, if the man who professes to be God's messenger has failed to declare to his hearers the truth of God as it is in Christ Jesus, those who have heard him will perish under the wrath of God, and he will perish with them! (1 Cor. 9:16; cf. Ezek: 33:8). In that awesome hour the unsaved church member will look into the face of his unsaved pastor, and with the smoke of hell in his lungs and the hatred of hell in his heart, he will cry, 'Why, why didn't you tell me the truth? My blood is upon your head!' And both of them will be cast together into hell.

Let no man dare stand in the pulpit to speak to men and women in God's name who is not prepared to stand before the judgement bar of God to give an account for having done so.

The apostle Paul was fully aware of these awesome realities when he stood before the Ephesian elders. Knowing that he would never see their faces again until they met before the judgement seat, Paul called for those who had heard him preach to bear witness of his faithfulness as a watchman. He said, 'I take you to record this day, that I am pure from the blood of all men. For I have not shunned to declare unto you all the counsel of God' (Acts 20:26-27). This was not an arrogant boast, but a statement of truth. Without courting the approval or fearing the disapproval of any, Paul had plainly declared to all who heard him the truth of God; and, having preached the truth of God to all who heard him, Paul was free from the blood of all. In the Day of Judgement no one will be able to look at Paul and say, 'I am damned because of you. You did not show me the way of life. You valued my approval, my friendship and my favour more than you valued my soul. My blood is upon your hands! Why didn't you tell me the truth?'

Using Paul as an example and the words of God to Ezekiel as our standard, I want us to see from the Word of God three tests of a true watchman. If we care for our own souls, we will test and prove every preacher we hear (1 John 4:1-3). The way to prove a preacher's faithfulness to our souls is by the Word of God, by the message he preaches, not by our own feelings and opinions. The test of a watchman is his faithfulness in keeping watch over the souls of his hearers, warning them of danger and showing them the way of life, by preaching the gospel of Christ to them.

The watchman's work

The work of a watchman is not complicated, mysterious, or hard to discern. He has only one thing to do: he must keep watch over the camp. God says, 'Thou shalt hear the word at my mouth, and warn them from me.' That is simple enough. When Paul gave account of his ministry, he simply declared, 'I have not shunned to declare unto you all the counsel of God.' In other words, he said, 'The word which I received from God I preached to you. I kept back nothing.' This is the whole work of the ministry. A faithful pastor is a man who diligently seeks a word from God for his people and faithfully delivers that word.

It is a watchman's responsibility to keep his post. His commander may move him from one place to another at his discretion, but the watchman's duty is always the same. God may move his servants from one place to another, but their work never varies. The pastor is a watchman. He must not be moved from his post by any fear, intimidation, allurement, or personal desire. He must give himself entirely to the work of the ministry (1 Tim. 4:12-16). He must separate himself from all other things and give himself wholly to the work of the gospel ministry.

Faithful pastors are men who labour in the gospel. As John Gill says, 'They are not loiterers, slothful servants, who hide their talents in a napkin and may be called idle shepherds, sleeping, lying down, loving to slumber, who serve not the Lord Jesus, nor the souls of men. But faithful ministers are labourers, [they] labour in the word and doctrine, and so are worthy of double honour.'

Every pastor must give himself relentlessly to the work of the ministry. Satan will use every means imaginable to distract him from it, if he can. But the pastor must not be distracted from the work he is called to do. Day by day, he must resolutely give himself to the work of the gospel. Though he is a citizen, he cannot be given to politics. Though he is a husband, he cannot give himself to his wife. Though he is a father, he cannot give himself to his family. He must give himself only to Christ and the gospel of his grace. The souls of men, the glory of Christ and the truth of God are at stake!

The pastor must relentlessly give himself to the study of Holy Scripture, ever seeking to know and understand the Word of God. He must be a man of earnest prayer, depending upon the Lord, interceding for God's elect, seeking a message from God, and praying for grace and power from God to deliver his message to the hearts of those who hear him. He must preach the gospel of Christ with untiring zeal. First and foremost, the pastor must be a preacher, a man separated to the gospel, using every gift and opportunity and means God gives him to preach the gospel. His time, his pen and his voice must be used for the furtherance of the gospel. Pastor, 'Meditate upon these things; give thyself wholly to them.'

It is the responsibility of every pastor, as a watchman, to proclaim to all men the Word of God, to preach to all 'all the counsel of God' (2 Tim. 4:1-5). What did Paul mean when he said, 'I have not shunned to declare unto you all the counsel of God'? He did not mean, 'I have declared to you all the secret decrees of God.' No man knows God's secret decrees. Nor did he mean, 'I have expounded to you every text of the Bible.' That could hardly have been done in three years! When Paul said, 'I have not shunned to declare unto you all the counsel of God,' his meaning was, 'I have faithfully preached in your hearing the whole body of divine truth. I have preached to you the whole gospel of Jesus Christ' (1 Peter 1:25). Paul told the Corinthians the very same thing, when he said, 'I determined to know nothing among you, save Jesus Christ, and him crucified' (1 Cor. 2:2). Christ crucified, the gospel of God's free grace to sinners upon the merits of Christ's obedience, is the whole counsel of God.

To preach all the counsel of God is to declare to all men, at all times, the vital truths of the gospel, to keep back nothing that is profitable to the souls of men. Sitting around a table one evening with a group of preachers, I was asked, 'How often do you preach "the five points"?' I think the man was insinuating that, perhaps, I preach the doctrines of grace too much. Without a second's hesitation, I responded, 'Every time I preach.' And I was not exaggerating! It is my full conviction that every time a man stands to preach in God's name it is his responsibility to preach all the counsel of God, to tell perishing sinners everything they must know to exercise saving faith in the Lord Jesus Christ.

Men must be told of God's glorious majesty as God, if they are to worship him as God. They must be told of his total sovereignty, his absolute holiness, his inflexible justice and his infinite goodness. Sinners must be informed of their desperate need as helpless, totally depraved, guilty and condemned felons before this holy Lord God, for no one will come to Christ until he knows his need of Christ. Men and women must have the wondrous mystery of redemption preached to them if they are to believe on the Lord Jesus Christ. No one can trust an unknown Saviour, and Christ cannot be known apart from the preaching of the gospel (Rom. 10:14-17). His representative obedience, substitutionary atonement and effectual grace must be fully preached. No one can be saved until he or she understands that 'Salvation is of the Lord!' I fully agree with Rowland Hill, who said, 'Any sermon that does not contain the three 'R's of the gospel (Ruin by the Fall, Redemption by the blood and Regeneration by the Holy Spirit) ought never to have been preached.'

To preach all the counsel of God is to preach Christ, only Christ, all of Christ and nothing but Christ all the time! Doctrine divorced from Christ is nothing but dead, religious philosophy. Duty divorced from Christ is nothing but self-righteous legalism. Devotion divorced from Christ is nothing but superstition. Christ is the subject of all biblical truth. Christ is the fulfilment of all biblical prophecy. Christ is the end of all biblical law. Christ is the motive of all biblical precepts. Christ is the example of all biblical standards. Christ is the foundation of all biblical hope. And Christ is the reward of all biblical faith. In a word, in all true gospel preaching, 'Christ is all.'

It is the responsibility of the watchman to press upon all who hear him the claims of Christ in the gospel (2 Cor. 5:10-21). God's servants know and preach all the glorious gospel truths of divine sovereignty, absolute predestination, eternal election, limited atonement, irresistible grace and immutable preservation. If any sinner is saved, it will be God's doing, only God's doing. With equal emphasis they declare the responsibility of all to trust Christ. God commands all to believe the gospel and promises salvation and eternal life to all who trust his Son, the Lord Jesus Christ. If anyone goes to hell, it will be his own fault, only his own fault (Prov. 1:23-33; Matt. 11:25-30; 23:37-38).

The watchman must declare the truth of God in plain, clear, unmistakable terms. Not only must the preacher preach the truth; he must preach it with such simplicity and clarity that no one can mistake his meaning. Paul said, 'I take you to record,' that is to say, 'You who have heard me know and bear witness of what I have preached to you.' Someone said, 'The gospel must be declared plainly, without disguise; fully, without concealment; firmly, without doubt; authoritatively, without fear.'

This is the watchman's work. He must not sleep at his post. He must not be enticed to leave his work or neglect it by any means. He must not be driven from his post by any trouble or fear. God holds him accountable.

The watchman's worth

Would to God that every believer knew the worth of that man who is God's faithful watchman over his soul! In and of himself the watchman is worthless, and he knows it (Rom. 7:18; Eph. 3:8). Like those to whom he preaches, he is but a fallen, depraved son of Adam, a sinful wretch, but if he is a faithful watchman his value cannot be calculated. His work is the most important work in the world. By faithful obedience to the work God has committed to his hands, the watchman shall both save himself and those who hear him (1 Tim.

4:16). That man who faithfully preaches the gospel of Christ to you is the instrument of God by which you have eternal life. He has no power or ability to save, but without the message he preaches you could not be saved. Such a man is to be highly honoured and esteemed for his work's sake (1 Thess. 5:12-13). Such a man is to be highly valued (Isa. 52:7). You cannot honour him too highly, or value him too greatly.

The watchman's witness

As we have already seen, every faithful pastor will have to give account before God and bear witness at the bar of God's judgement, regarding those for whom he is a watchman (Heb. 13:17). With joy, he will confess that those who believed his message obeyed the gospel. But, with grief, he will bear witness against all who heard the message of God's free grace in Christ and refused to believe. Let every watchman be faithful to his work, and let all who hear the Word of God from the mouth of his watchman obey the gospel.

Several years ago a man slipped into the auditorium as I began to preach one Tuesday evening. I had never seen him before. One of our men worked with him, and had invited him to come and hear the preaching of the gospel. That night, I preached the message God had given me. The man made little comment as he left the building. On Wednesday morning he went out for his usual walk, and suddenly, unexpectedly, he fell over dead by the roadside. His time was up, and God took him. I do not know whether the man was converted by the message he heard, but I do know this: I am free of his blood. I preached to him all the counsel of God that Tuesday night. And at the last day, I will give witness before God, either of his faith or his unbelief; and he will testify that he heard God's gospel from the voice of a watchman. Had I failed to be a watchman to his soul, had I failed to warn him of his way and show him Christ the Way, I could not sleep at night for fear of seeing his face again at the judgement.

6.
What should I do for my pastor?

*'How beautiful upon the mountains are the feet of him that bringeth
good tidings, that publisheth peace; that bringeth good tidings of
good, that publisheth salvation; that saith unto Zion, Thy God
reigneth!'* (Isa. 52:7).

I have described, as plainly and fully as I can, the responsibilities of
gospel preachers to the church of God. In this chapter I want to show
the reader the responsibilities of God's people to their pastors. We
shall begin our study in Isaiah 52:7. Here the prophet of God
describes the attitude which ought to prevail in the hearts of God's
saints towards those men who are sent of God to preach the gospel
to them.

The picture is of a city in captivity which begins to rejoice as she
hears the sound of an army coming across the mountains to deliver
her. The church of God's elect is by nature in captivity, taken captive
by Satan, held in the bondage of sin and shut up under the curse of
God's holy law. God's servants are an army of men, coming over the
mountains, proclaiming deliverance by our great God and Saviour,
the Lord Jesus Christ, and they are highly valued by those who know
their need of deliverance by Christ. Those men and women who
have heard and experienced the salvation of God in Christ cherish
the men who are sent of God to proclaim deliverance to their hearts.

Look again at the prophet's words. By divine inspiration Isaiah
speaks as the representative of God's church: 'How beautiful upon
the mountains are the feet of him that bringeth good tidings, that

publisheth peace; that bringeth good tidings of good, that publisheth salvation; that saith unto Zion, Thy God reigneth!' Obviously, these words do not apply to every man who calls himself a preacher and claims to come in the name of the Lord. False prophets, preachers of free-will, works religion, are not beautiful or desirable, for they do not bring good news. They are not to be treated with respect, but with contempt. They are not to be received, but shunned. Isaiah tells us plainly who those preachers are whose feet are beautiful, whose coming is desirable to the church of God. They are the men who are sent of God to preach the everlasting gospel of his free, sovereign, saving grace in Christ (Rom. 10:15).

They bring good tidings! They bring good tidings from the heart of God to the hearts of needy sinners, declaring that righteousness is established and redemption is accomplished for all who believe by the Lord Jesus Christ (Rom. 10:4; Heb. 9:12).

They publish peace! God's servants never tell helpless sinners to make peace with God. How can a traitor, a rebel, a felon make peace with the sovereign he has offended? If peace is made it must be made by the sovereign. God's servants proclaim that peace has been made for sinners by the Lord Jesus Christ (2 Cor. 5:18-21; Isa. 40:1-2).

They bring good tidings of good! God's preachers do not offer good advice. They proclaim good news. Justice is satisfied! Atonement is made! Redemption is finished! Sin has been put away! God is reconciled! God forgives sin! God accepts sinners! God is merciful to the guilty! God saves graciously! God freely receives sinners as objects of his everlasting love through faith in the blood and righteousness of his dear Son, the sinner's substitute, Jesus Christ! (Rom. 3:19-28).

They publish salvation! Gospel preachers do not tell helpless, depraved, dead sinners what they must do to save themselves. They proclaim to the helplessly lost sons of Adam how that God sovereignly saves his elect for the glory of his grace by blood atonement, imputed righteousness and effectual power (Ps. 65:4; 110:3; Rom. 5:12-21; Eph. 1:3-14; 2:1-10).

They say unto Zion, 'Thy God reigneth!' Every man who is sent of

God as a messenger of grace to needy sinners proclaims, in clear and unmistakable terms, the glorious, absolute and universal sovereignty of God in creation (Gen. 1:1), providence (Rom. 8:28; 11:36) and grace (Rom. 9:11-23). 'Our God is in the heavens; he hath done whatsoever he hath pleased' (Ps. 115:3). 'Whatsoever the Lord pleased, that did he in heaven, and in earth, in the seas, and all deep places' (Ps. 135:6). Every message from every faithful gospel preacher sets forth the glorious sovereignty of God.

Any man who does not preach these things is not sent of God and must not be received, heard, or aided in any way by God's church (2 John 9-11). Any man who does preach these things is to be heard and received by the church of God and treated as the angel of God among them. He is God's messenger.

If you know the value of your soul, the preciousness of Christ and his blood and the blessedness of the gospel, you will cherish that man who is sent of God to preach the gospel to you. You want to treat him as the messenger of God to your soul and do everything you can for him. If you are reading these pages, I am sure you are very interested in the answer to this question: 'What should I do for my pastor?' I have searched the Scriptures and found ten answers to that question. Here are ten things revealed in the Word of God which every church and every believer within the church should do for the man who preaches the gospel of Christ to them, labouring for their souls' eternal good.

1. Know him (1 Thess. 5:12)

Obviously, this means more than having a bare acquaintance with him. It is unthinkable that a church might have a pastor with whom it is unacquainted. To know your pastor is to *acknowledge him as your pastor*, as the messenger of God to your soul. Every believer should get to know, and show his care for, every faithful pastor, preacher, missionary and evangelist that he can. God's people need to build strong relationships with God's servants everywhere. I pastor a local church, and I highly encourage the people of our assembly to write to, visit and get to know every faithful gospel preacher they can. (God's servants are not jealous or fearful of one another!) But there should be a special relationship between a pastor and the congregation which he serves. Your pastor is to be acknowledged by you, above all others, as God's messenger to you. That makes him special to you.

To know your pastor is to *love him*. The word 'know' is often used for 'love' in the Scriptures, and every member of the church should have a distinct love for the man who is the instrument of God to minister to the needs of his people. The man who devotes his life to securing your soul's comfort, edification and strength is worthy of your love.

To know your pastor is to *hold him in respect*. Paul admonished the Philippians to hold their pastor in reputation, to honour him (Phil. 2:29). God's people are to give honour to those men who are God's ambassadors. They are to be treated as God's ambassadors (Luke 10:16).

To know your pastor is to *show concern for his comfort, welfare, safety and protection*. David used the word 'know' in this way (Ps. 142:4). Churches should be greatly concerned for the safety and welfare of their pastors in the discharge of their responsibilities. Pray for your pastor's spiritual safety and well-being. Protect his name and reputation from the slanderous gossip of evil men, and always endeavour to encourage him in his work.

Paul gives three reasons why churches should make it their business to know their pastors.

1. They labour among you. If God has given you a faithful pastor, he has given you a man who labours for your soul. He fills his hours with diligent work, studying hard, praying earnestly, preaching fervently. He corresponds with needy people. He visits the sick. He writes articles, tracts, books, etc. The vast majority of his work is unseen by those for whom it is done, and too often unappreciated. But faithful pastors are labouring pastors.

2. They are over you by divine appointment. God has placed your pastor over you as your spiritual guide and ruler in his kingdom. If you would follow his faith, you need to know him.

3. They admonish you. Your pastor continually reminds you, in public and in private, of things which you need to know. He reminds you of your past experiences of grace (Isa. 50:1-2). He faithfully preaches and instructs you in the doctrines of the gospel (1 Cor. 1:26-31; Rom. 8:28-39). He reminds you of your privileges and responsibilities in this world (Eph. 4:17-5:2). He points out the dangers you must face (Matt. 13:18-23). Finally, he ever reminds you of the blessed, soul-cheering promises of God in Christ (Isa. 43:1-5; 2 Cor. 1:20).

2. Esteem him very highly (1 Thess. 5:13)

Every believer should esteem his pastor very highly. The word is 'superabundantly', over and above the esteem given to other' brothers and sisters in Christ. This is not because he possesses any personal superiority; he does not. He, like you, is 'only a sinner saved by grace'. But he is to be esteemed superabundantly for his work's sake. What does this mean?

You are to *entertain the highest possible opinions of your pastor* at all times. Hold him up in your own mind. Highly esteem his gifts and abilities as a preacher, and his grace and faithfulness as a believer. If you have a low opinion of a man, it is not likely that he will be of much use to your soul. His words will carry no weight with you.

Always *speak honourably of your pastor*. Believers should always speak well of one another, but this is especially true regarding their pastors. If you do not speak well of your pastor, it is not likely that anyone who knows you will have any respect for him. At home, among the members of your family, at work, in the midst of your co-workers and in the community, always give God's servant the highest possible esteem in your speech.

Speak respectfully to your pastor as God's messenger to you. The use of titles and names of distinction to separate and elevate God's servants above his people is to be deplored. Our Lord plainly forbids it (Matt. 23:7-9). We should address no man as 'Reverend', 'Father', or 'Doctor'! But God's servants should be spoken to in respectful terms. Neither the pastor's office nor his work should be made the object of a joke or of ridicule. Like a father in his household, the pastor is to be treated and spoken to with the respect that becomes his high and holy office in the church.

This superabundant esteem must be the esteem of sincere love for the pastor's work's sake. It is not a forced reverence for an office. It is to be a heartfelt esteem flowing from your realization of the burden, labour and value of the work of the gospel, to which God's servant faithfully gives himself. That man deserves your highest, most loving esteem who spends his life in ardent labour for the gospel, who has been the instrument used of God for your salvation, who ministers to the comfort of your soul and is used of God for your spiritual growth and edification in the knowledge of Christ.

3. Remember him (Heb. 13:7)

Ever keep your pastor close to your heart in fond remembrance. Remember him at the throne of grace when you pray, but particularly, the admonition here is to remember his messages and the doctrine he preaches. Listen carefully to what he preaches. Take notes to aid your memory. Discuss his sermons at home, among your brethren, and store up his doctrine in your mind, so that you may apply it to yourself as you seek to live in this world for the glory of God. As you read the Word of God in your private worship, if you remember what has been preached to you the Word will open before you and be blessed of God to your heart.

Here are two reasons for remembering your pastor, particularly, for remembering his messages. Firstly, he has the rule of the church. His word is to be remembered, because God has made him your spiritual guide in this world, and, secondly, he speaks to you the Word of God. He does not come in his own name, teaching his own opinions, or the philosophies of men. If he is God's man, your pastor comes to you with God's message, armed with God's authority, and what he says you are responsible to hear, remember and obey. He preaches to you the Word of God.

4. Follow him (Heb. 13:7)

Believers and churches are to follow their pastors. Your pastor is your leader and guide in the kingdom of God. You are to follow his example of faith and faithfulness. Follow the pure gospel doctrine that he preaches to you. It leads to life everlasting. Follow his example of devotion to Christ. Your pastor, if he is truly the servant of God, is a man of resolute, heart devotion to Christ, his church, his gospel and his glory. He guides God's people by his own example of consecration to Christ. Follow his example of faithfulness. The one thing God requires of his servants is faithfulness, and if you would be serviceable to the cause of Christ in your own sphere of responsibility, you will learn how by following your pastor's example.

This is not blind allegiance to a man. This is obedience to Christ. If you would follow Christ, you must follow the man he has made your guide, considering the end of his conversation, 'Jesus Christ the same yesterday, and today, and for ever' (Heb. 13:8). Christ is the object of our faith, the pattern of our faith and the end of our faith. Follow your pastor in the life of faith, as he presses towards the mark, Christ Jesus.

5. Obey him (Heb. 13:17)

Obedience is not servitude, but it does mean submission. God's people are expected and required to obey their pastors. In spiritual, doctrinal matters, in all things regarding the affairs and work of the church, the pastor is to be obeyed. If he is not worthy of obedience, he should not be the pastor. Elders are to serve the church in obedience to the pastor. Deacons are to serve the church in obedience to the pastor. Teachers are to serve the church in obedience to the pastor. Every member of the congregation is to serve the church in obedience to the pastor. The pastor is the captain of the ship. All the crew must serve in obedience to him.

Obey his message, the gospel of the grace of God. Hear it. Receive it. Love it, and order your life by it.

Obey his direction in the worship of Christ. Every aspect of the worship and work of the church should be carried out in accordance with the pastor's instruction. The order of the services, the selection of music, the administration of the ordinances and the activities of the church are to be performed in the way required by the pastor, as he is guided by the Word of God. There is no need for committees and societies within the church body. The pastor's voice, as he seeks the will and glory of God, is to be obeyed in all things.

Obey his admonitions and reproofs. No pastor is infallible. He will often err. But if he is a faithful man, his errors will be errors of judgement, not errors of principle. You can safely follow such a man and obey him. His admonitions and reproofs, if he is God's servant, are not personal attacks, or fits of passion. They are thoughtful, needful, God-given warnings and directions for your soul's eternal good.

6. Submit to him (Heb. 13:17)

The admonition here is to submit yourself to the Spirit-led, faithful care of your pastor. Do what he tells you to do, even if you do not really understand why. That may seem a little too much to expect, but a little consideration will show that it is not.

A few years ago, I was dying with cancer. The doctors wanted to treat my disease by injecting me with a series of drugs and cobalt treatments. The drugs and the treatments could prove deadly themselves, if they were not properly administered. I do not understand how they work, but, being confident of my physicians' abilities, I submitted myself to them and did what they told me to do, because I knew that they knew better than I did what was needed.

You are to submit to your pastor in just that way. If he is a faithful man, he probably knows better than you what is best for your soul, the cause of Christ, the welfare of the church and the furtherance of the gospel. He will not wilfully mislead you, and he will not abuse you, or take advantage of you.

Your pastor's concern is for the welfare of your soul. He watches for your soul as one who must give account, both to his own conscience and at the judgement bar of God. Every faithful pastor exercises great care and diligence as he watches over God's people, for he desires to give account of his hearers with joy and not with grief. If on the Day of Judgement God's servant gives account of you with grief, as one who has heard but refused to obey the gospel, you will suffer the wrath of God for it (Deut. 17:11-12).

7. Pray for him (Eph. 6:19: Col. 4:3; 2 Thess. 3:1)

Let every child of God pray continually for all who faithfully preach the gospel of Christ, but every believer should especially pray for his own pastor. C. H. Spurgeon was once asked, 'To what do you attribute the phenomenal success of your ministry?' Without a

moment's hesitation, he replied, 'My people pray for me.' Let all
who believe follow their example. Pray for your pastor. As he seeks
a message for your soul in his private study and preparation for the
pulpit, pray for him. As he preaches the gospel to you, pray for him.
Pray, too, for your pastor with regard to his life and conduct in this
world. He is a man, like yourself, weak, frail, sinful and tempted of
the devil. Pray for his preservation from the evil one. Pray that God
will ever give him grace to seek neither to avoid the disfavour of
men, nor to crave the favour of men. Call upon God to preserve him
in grace, in usefulness and in health and strength, and pray for your
pastor's constant and increasing usefulness in the cause of Christ.

8. Provide for him (1 Tim. 5:17-18; Gal. 6:6; 1 Cor. 9:7-14)

Carefully read these texts of Scripture. Then read them again and ask
the Spirit of God to apply them to your own heart. It is a shame and
reproach upon any congregation which is able to care for its pastor,
if the pastor has to provide for any of his own, or his family's earthly,
material needs. And it is the congregation itself which suffers when
the pastor has to support himself.

Every local church should generously supply every need of the
pastor and his family, so that he may be able to give himself wholly
to prayer, study and preaching. A faithful man will make whatever
sacrifices and adjustments are necessary to live within his means,
and he will not take advantage of the generosity of God's people.
But every church, and every member of the church, should do
everything within its ability to see to it that God's servant lacks for
nothing.

9. Adhere to him (2 Tim. 1:15-18)

In every state, condition and circumstance, adhere to your pastor. He
needs you. In difficulty, support him. When he is discouraged,
encourage him. When he is engaged in trials, sympathize with him.
When he is opposed, stand by him. When men speak evil of him,
defend him. In all his labour for Christ, your soul and the gospel of
the grace of God, do whatever you can to assist him, for the glory of
God.

10. Treat him as the minister of Christ (1 Cor. 4:1-2)

He has been made your minister for Christ's sake by the will of God. He is the steward of the mysteries of God. God has made him the servant in his house who is entrusted with the treasury of the house, the gospel of the grace of God. And, if he is God's servant, he is faithful to your soul in all things.

We have seen, from the Word of God, ten things which the believer should be doing for his pastor. Many will say, 'No man deserves to be treated so royally,' and, of course, they are right. No man *deserves* to have such treatment from his peers. But if God's servants are to be effective in, and give themselves, to the work of the gospel, they must have the unwavering help, support and faithfulness of God's people behind them. Remember also that your pastor, if he is God's faithful servant, is God's ambassador to your soul; and the Lord regards that which is done to his ambassadors, be it good or bad, as having been done to him (Luke 10:16).

Churches sometimes wonder why they cannot keep a pastor more than a few years. There may be many reasons. But this one thing I have observed, after a good many years of pastoral experience: very few pastors would even consider the possibility of leaving any church which did for them the things which we have seen in this chapter. Personally, I have never known a pastor to leave such a congregation. If you would do what is right, and if you would keep your pastor, these are the things you should be doing for him.

7.
The elders of the church

'And from Miletus he sent to Ephesus, and called the elders of the church' (Acts 20:17).

What is an elder? What does he do? Very few Baptists know the answers to these questions. In most Baptist churches the term 'elder' is ambiguous. Very few know its significance, because most Baptist churches long ago dispensed with the office of the elder. Today, these churches are usually governed purely by the will of the people, without regard to the Word of God. At appointed times the church meets for business and the people decide every issue. Man-made rules of order have replaced the leadership of the Holy Spirit. The opinion of the majority takes precedence over the Word of God, and the will of the people overrules the will of God. The congregation votes to hire a preacher, tell him what he is expected to do, when, where and how long he can preach, and appoint a board of deacons to watch over the preacher, making certain that he does what he was hired to do. But in the New Testament it was not so.

The church of the New Testament is a spiritual society, governed by the Spirit of God, according to the Word of God, through the instrumentality of God-ordained, God-given elders and deacons.

Deacons are godly men, men full of the Holy Spirit, ordained and given by God to his church to relieve gospel preachers of all mundane, material, monetary concerns (Acts 6:2-7). Deacons may, or may not, be gifted to preach and teach. Some are; some are not. But deacons are not responsible for the government and spiritual oversight of the church. Deacons are responsible for the honest and faithful distribution of church funds, the maintenance and care of church property and the material needs of pastors, missionaries, widows and orphans.

Elders are men called and gifted of God to rule over, lead, guide and govern his house by the Word of God. The elders of a local church are 'the presbytery', or ruling body of the church (1 Tim. 4:14). The elders of the church are those men God has appointed, gifted and qualified to serve as the spiritual rulers of his house. The qualifications required of an elder are exactly the same as those required of a pastor (1 Tim. 3:1-7; Titus 1:5-9). In fact, as we shall see from the Scriptures, the pastor is an elder, the presiding elder of the presbytery.

At the outset, let me make this clear: I do not suggest, or imply, that a local church must have more than one elder, any more than it must have a board of deacons, in order for it to be a properly constituted church. The New Testament makes no such requirement. In fact, small, young churches seldom need either a board of elders or a board of deacons. The pastor can manage the affairs of such congregations himself. But as the church grows and assumes greater responsibilities and its ministry is enlarged by God's providence, the pastor must have gifted men to assist him in the work of the ministry. As the need arises for deacons, God will provide suitable men to serve as deacons. As the need arises for elders, God will provide suitable men to serve as elders. But neither elders nor deacons should be ordained and appointed to an office for which there is no need. In Acts 6 there was a need in the church, and at the time of need seven faithful men were provided by the Lord.

There are four things clearly revealed in the New Testament about the elders of the church.

1. Elders are the spiritual rulers of the local church

The church of God is a society of regenerated men and women, brought together by the Spirit of God for the worship of Christ and the preaching of the gospel. God's church in this world exists for and is dedicated to three things.

1. *We seek the glory of God our Saviour, the Lord Jesus Christ.* This must be our primary concern in all things, that Christ may both be pre-eminent and be glorified (Col. 1:18; 1 Cor. 1:29, 31). We must embrace no doctrine but that which glorifies Christ. We are to practise no ordinances but those which Christ has given for the celebration of his praise — baptism and the Lord's Supper — and we are to observe them precisely as our Lord prescribes in his Word. We are to engage in no activities other than those which promote the worship of, and obedience to, Christ. There is no room in the church of God for entertainment, social clubs or anything that has nothing to do with preaching the gospel and the worship of our Lord.

2. *We are dedicated to the preaching of the gospel of God's free and sovereign grace in Christ* (1 Cor. 9:16; 1 Tim. 3:15). Let others deride preaching, if they will. Let others belittle the preaching of the gospel of God's grace, if they dare. Let others relegate preaching to a fifteen or twenty minute segment of the Sunday programme, if they hold it in such contempt. God's church has no other purpose for existence in this world than preaching, and it has no message but the free and sovereign grace of God in Jesus Christ. To the preaching of Christ crucified, we must be committed. Ignorant men may call the preaching of the gospel 'riding a hobby horse', 'ranting about Calvinism' or 'bigoted dogmatism', but we must not be deterred. It is the responsibility of every gospel preacher and every local church to preach the gospel of Christ unceasingly and without apology, and it is our responsibility to lay particular emphasis upon those vital points of gospel doctrine which men most oppose. We must preach grace alone, sovereign electing grace, sovereign redeeming grace, sovereign saving grace, sovereign preserving grace!

3. *We are committed to the salvation of God's elect* (2 Tim. 2:10). We are not to seek recognition, approval, or applause from men; we are to seek the salvation of God's elect through the preaching of the gospel.

These are to be our goals. Because we seek things which do not in any way depend upon men, things which God alone can accomplish, and which we know God will accomplish, we shall never need to court men or compromise the Word of God. But what do these things have to do with elders being the spiritual rulers of the church? Let me explain.

In order to accomplish her God-given mission, in order to accomplish those goals, *the local church must have God-given rulers.* Every orderly society must have rulers. Someone has to give direction with authority; otherwise there will be nothing but chaos, confusion and strife. Many churches are constantly torn with strife, primarily because no one is in charge. Our Lord is not the author of confusion. Therefore he has given elders to rule his house (1 Thess. 5:12-13; Heb. 13:7, 17, 24). *OVER Seeks ELDERS RULE BY to Be OBEYED. The Gospel*

The elders of the church do not rule by any arbitrary authority, but by the authority of Holy Scripture. They do not formulate doctrines, or enact laws. They simply proclaim the Word of God to his people. The elders' authority is not personal; it is ministerial. They rule not by force, but by preaching the gospel.

God's saints are obliged to follow and obey their elders as they follow Christ. I know there is a danger of men abusing their place in the kingdom of God. But one man's disobedience will not make another obey, and any attempt to regulate the elders' authority beyond the Scriptures cannot be tolerated. Any church that earnestly seeks to obey the Scriptures will enjoy the protection of God's Spirit. Just as God protected Israel from wicked kings, he will protect his church from wicked men who abuse the elders' office. It is the elders' responsibility to rule and the church's responsibility to follow. An elder has no power to force obedience, but the power of God's Spirit; and the church has no power to control the elder, but the power of God's Spirit. In both cases, the Spirit of God does a much better job than the efforts of men! Elders must take the oversight of God's flock, without imposing their own will upon the flock (Acts 20:28; 1 Peter 5:1-3); and the church is to obey willingly the lead, direction, guidance and rule of those elders who faithfully instruct them in the Word of God.

Every elder must gain and keep the respect and esteem of the church by his example of leadership (1 Peter 5:3). Those who rule the house of God rule by the authority of God's Word, but they must earn the right to rule over men by their example of faith, faithfulness and obedience. No elder has any right to expect men and women to be or do anything which he does not show them how to be and do by his example. If he calls for men to be patient in trial, he must show patience. If he calls for others to obey God, he must show obedience.

If he calls men to devotion, he must exemplify devotion. If he calls for commitment, he must exemplify commitment. If he asks men and women to be sacrificial, he must lead them by example. The word we preach will have no power over men unless it is enforced by our personal example.

2. Elders are known by various titles in the Scriptures

We usually think of an elder as an older man, but, as it is used in the New Testament, the word really does not imply a man's age. It implies dignity, maturity, sober-mindedness, experience and wisdom. An elder in the church is a man of spiritual maturity, experience, wisdom and stability. An elder must not be a novice, but he may be a young man (1 Tim. 4:12).

Sometimes elders are called 'pastors' (Eph. 4:11). The word 'pastor' means 'shepherd'. Elders are shepherds, men responsible for the care, protection, direction and feeding of Christ's sheep.

Sometimes they are called 'bishops' (1 Tim. 3:1). A bishop is an overseer. He watches over other men, to make certain that the church of God fulfils the will of God, as prescribed in the Word of God. Like a foreman in a factory, the bishop is responsible to see that the church keeps to her God-given work.

Sometimes they are called 'elders' (Titus 1:5). Elders are mature, sober-minded, wise men who have won the respect of others. Their voice carries authority, because they speak with the wisdom of experience.

These three titles, pastor, bishop and elder, do not suggest three different offices in the church. They refer to one office. Pastors are bishops and elders in the church of God.

3. The New Testament shows a plurality of elders in each local church

I cannot find a single place in the New Testament where a local church existed with only one elder. God does not tell us that each church must have more than one, but the Scriptures certainly imply that ideally every well-established church is to have a plurality of elders. Let us look at some scriptures and see if this is not the case.

In Acts 14:21-23 Paul and Barnabas returned to the churches of Lystra, Iconium, and Antioch, confirming the disciples in the faith and exhorting them to steadfastness in the gospel, and they ordained 'elders in every church'. When these churches were younger and smaller, they did not need a plurality of elders. But once they were established and strong more than one elder was required.

In Acts 20:17 Paul gathered 'the elders of the church' at Ephesus and gave them his final charge before departing for Jerusalem. The church at Ephesus had a plurality of elders.

In 1 Timothy 5:17 the apostle wrote, 'Let the elders [plural] that rule well be counted worthy of double honour, especially they who labour in the word and doctrine.'

Paul left Titus in Crete to set things in order in the churches 'and ordain elders in every city' (Titus 1:5). One part of setting things in order was the ordination of elders in every church.

James instructs sick believers to 'call for the elders of the church; and let them pray over him, anointing him with oil in the name of the Lord' (James 5:14). Not one is to be called, but the elders are to be called. Not one is to pray, but *they* are to pray. Not one is to anoint the sick, but *they* are to anoint the sick one.

Peter addressed himself to 'the elders' among the flock of God, urging them to be 'ensamples to the flock' (1 Peter 5:1-3).

In every place where churches and elders are spoken of, elders are spoken of as being plural. We are never told how many elders a congregation might have, or how many one should have, but that every church had more than one elder is obvious.

4. There must always be one presiding elder, responsible for the doctrinal, spiritual oversight of the church

Someone has to be in charge of things. Two men cannot take the helm of one ship, hold the reins of one horse, or have the pastoral charge of one church. It may appear pious and spiritual for two or more men to talk of being 'co-pastors' in a church. But it is not possible. More importantly, it is not biblical. There can only be one pastor in a congregation.

We have already seen that the pastor is an elder, but the Scriptures do distinguish between the pastor and the other elders of the congregation. In every local church there is one pastor-teacher, under whose direction all the other elders and the deacons serve the church (Eph. 4:11). There may be many elders in the church, but there can only be one pastor-teacher. All the elders serve with the pastor, but they all must serve under the pastor. Otherwise there will be confusion and chaos.

This principle holds true in every aspect of life. Two people cannot be in charge of one thing. God has appointed two parents in a household. The mother is to be respected and obeyed by the children, but she is not the head of the house. She serves with her husband in the government of the house, but she serves under him as her head. There are two pilots on a passenger aircraft, but one of them is responsible for flying the plane. He is the captain. The other man is capable of flying the plane. He is always there in case he is needed, but he keeps his hands off the controls unless the captain gives him orders to fly. Even then, the captain tells the co-pilot what bearings to keep. The welfare of the plane, passengers and crew, is the captain's responsibility. There may be many elders in the church, but there is one man who is *the elder*, the pastor of the church (2 John 1; 3 John 1). The spiritual welfare, doctrinal instruction and ministry of the whole church, elders, deacons and congregation, is his responsibility.

Let me give two examples to demonstrate this fact, that there can only be one elder who speaks with authority as God's messenger in each local church.

1. *Each of the letters to the seven churches of Asia was addressed to the messenger in charge of that particular church* (Rev. 1:20; 2:1, 8, 12, 18; 3:1, 7, 14). The word 'angel' used in these scriptures does not refer to a celestial creature. The word simply means 'messenger'. And for each church there was one messenger, one man who received the word from God and was responsible to deliver that message to the church. Though there were many elders in the church at Ephesus (Acts 20:17), there was only one angel there (Rev. 2:1), one messenger, one pastor-teacher, charged with the responsibility of delivering God's message to his people.

Just as Aaron, the high priest in Israel, was responsible for the sanctuary, its service and the Levites who served with him and who were given to him to assist him in the service of the sanctuary (Num. 18:1-7), so the pastor-teacher of a local church is responsible for the

Numbers 18 v 5

ministry of the church and for the ministries of those elders who assist him in the service of the congregation.

2. *The apostle Paul divides the elders of the church into two categories.* In 1 Timothy 5:17 he says, 'Let the elders that rule well be counted worthy of double honour, especially they who labour in the word and doctrine.' Some elders in the church are expected only to assist in the rule of the church by assisting in the ministry of the Word. Others are expected to spend their lives labouring in the study of the Word and the doctrine of the gospel. It is not necessary that all the elders of the presbytery possess the same gifts for preaching and teaching. All are involved in the rule of the church, as assistants to the pastor. They aid him in the ministry of the Word and by their ministries aid him in the government of the church, but the pastor is the man who labours in the Word and doctrine, being gifted, called and ordained of God as God's messenger to his people. All the elders are to be honoured for their service, but those who are gifted as God's messengers to his churches are to be especially, or more highly, honoured because of the message they bear and their labour in it. All the Levites were to be honoured as God's servants, but Aaron was especially honoured as God's high priest, in charge of the sanctuary. The illustration is applicable to the elders and the pastor, though neither are priests. And as there was no cause for jealousy among the Levites or pride among the sons of Aaron, there is no cause for jealousy in other elders or pride on the part of the pastor. Both serve God in the place God has ordained, with the gifts God has given for the glory of Christ and the good of his people.

What, then, is the responsibility of the elders of the church? The primary and greatest work of elders is to hold up the hands of faithful pastors in the work of the gospel. As Aaron and Hur held up the hands of Moses before Israel (Exod. 17:8-16), so the elders of the church are to hold up the pastor's hands before the congregation of the Lord. Some may think that to submit to and support another man in this way is degrading and it may offend their pride. Aaron and Hur counted it their honour to hold up the hands of Moses, for three reasons. Firstly, he was God's messenger; secondly, he held God's rod, the symbol of his Word; and thirdly, by their holding up his hands Israel prevailed over her enemies. May the Lord be pleased to give his churches today faithful pastors like Moses and faithful elders like Aaron and Hur. With such pastors and such elders, the Amalekites will surely flee before us!

8.
The office of a deacon

'Likewise must the deacons be grave, not doubletongued, not given to much wine, not greedy of filthy lucre; holding the mystery of the faith in a pure conscience. And let these also first be proved; then let them use the office of a deacon, being found blameless. Even so must their wives be grave, not slanderers, sober, faithful in all things. Let the deacons be the husbands of one wife, ruling their children and their own houses well. For they that have used the office of a deacon well purchase to themselves a good degree, and great boldness in the faith which is in Christ Jesus' (1 Tim. 3:8-13).

God has ordained two abiding offices in the church: pastors, or elders, and deacons. The extraordinary offices of prophets and apostles ceased with the completion of God's revelation of himself in the Holy Scriptures. But the ordinary offices of the church, pastors and deacons, are perpetual, abiding gifts of Christ to his church. In this chapter we will study what the Scriptures teach about 'the office of a deacon'.

In 1 Timothy 3:8-13 the apostle Paul describes the character and conduct of those men who are qualified to serve as deacons in the church. And in Acts 6:1-7 the Holy Spirit shows us why the church needs deacons and what their responsibilities are. Though the word 'deacon' is not used in Acts 6, this is where the office began: 'And in those days, when the number of the disciples was multiplied, there arose a murmuring of the Grecians against the Hebrews, because their widows were neglected in the daily ministration. Then the twelve called the multitude of the disciples unto them and said, It is not reason that we should leave the word of God, and serve tables. Wherefore, brethren, look ye out among you seven men of honest report, full of the Holy Ghost and wisdom, whom we may appoint over this business. But we will give ourselves continually to prayer, and to the ministry of the word. And the saying pleased the whole multitude: and they chose Stephen, a man full of faith and of the Holy Ghost, and Philip, and Prochorus, and Nicanor, and Timon, and Parmenas, and Nicolas a proselyte of Antioch: whom they set before the apostles; and when they had prayed, they laid their hands on them. And the word of God increased; and the number of the disciples multiplied in Jerusalem greatly; and a great company of the priests were obedient to the faith.'

The church at Jerusalem had grown, in a very short time, from 120 to several thousand in number. Many estimate that the number of believers by this time exceeded 10,000! God had greatly blessed his Word. The gospel of Christ was triumphant over the hearts of men. And those early believers, though they were numbered in the thousands, were identified by brotherly love and mutual care for one another. They had all things in common. Many who had lands and property sold their estates and gave the money to the church, so that all might live with a measure of equality. Of course, such a large congregation included many who were poor, destitute and dependent upon the charity of others. These poor believers, particularly widows and orphans, were fed, clothed and housed by the rest of the church. Their daily needs were met by taking funds from the church treasury. But a problem arose: some of the Greek widows (Hellenistic Jews) were being neglected (at least, they thought they were being neglected), not receiving an equal share in daily compensation with those who were of pure Jewish descent.

Several things should be observed here.

1. *Though the church suffered much persecution, it continued to grow.* The blessings of God were upon his Word and upon his people. Like the church in Egypt, the more it was afflicted, the more it multiplied. The Word of God, the cause of Christ and the success of the gospel cannot be hindered. The powers of darkness and the gates of hell fall before Christ's advancing army. God's work is done by God's hand, in God's way, at God's time, and it cannot be resisted. The church of God grew mightily. Without programmes,

gimmicks, or entertainment, by the power of God, through the preaching of the gospel, the church grew.

2. *This marvellous increase of disciples became an occasion for strife and discord within the church.* Until this time the saints had been of one accord. They were one in heart, mind and purpose, as well as one in doctrine. But when they began to multiply they corrupted themselves. They increased in size, but not in service. They increased in numbers, but not in grace. They increased in riches, but not in joy. As Abraham and Lot found that when their families increased there was strife between their herdsmen, so it was in this early church. 'There arose a murmuring.' It was not an open falling out, but a secret strife.

3. *The strife was about money.* What a pity! The insignificant, trivial things of this world were the cause of strife between men and women who professed to be citizens of the heavenly Jerusalem. Money was the cause of a quarrel in the church of God! That is astonishing, yet it is common. This evil is so often repeated that it cannot be ignored. 'The love of money is the root of all evil.' Quarrels between husbands and wives are more often than not about money. Bad feelings between members of the same family are usually over money, property and family possessions. A split in a church nearly always begins with strife about money.

4. *It is evident that there has never been a pure and perfect church in this world, and there never will be.* The church of God is made up of redeemed sinners. Though redeemed by the blood of Christ and saved by the grace of God, we are still sinners. Any congregation made up of sinful men and women will, from time to time, have problems to face, deal with and overcome. But husbands and wives do not break up the family because they have a disagreement, and believers do not forsake the church because problems arise. If we love one another and seek the glory of Christ, we will work together to overcome those problems.

The church of God at Jerusalem had a problem. A division arose over the use of church funds. In order to solve this problem and to prevent it from arising again in the future, the apostles, under the direction of the Holy Spirit, created a new office in the church — the office of deacon. 'Seven men of honest report, full of the Holy Ghost and wisdom' were chosen to take care of the business of the church. These deacons were chosen to meet a specific need in the church. Seven were chosen because seven were needed, and those seven men were a great asset both to the church and to the apostles. Faithful deacons are assets to any congregation and to any pastor.

If we would understand the office of a deacon five questions need to be answered from the Word of God.

1. Why was the office of deacon established?

We must make sure that we understand that the apostles did not simply invent an office in the church as a matter of expediency. They did what they did under the influence and direction of God the Holy Spirit. Unlike the choosing of Matthias to be an apostle (Acts 1), this was an act inspired by God. We know that their decision to ordain deacons was divinely inspired because it is confirmed in the epistles (1 Tim. 3:8-13).

God ordained the office of deacon, and he ordained it for a specific purpose. Deacons are to relieve God's servants of all secular, worldly, financial concern, so that they may give themselves entirely to the ministry of the Word (1 Tim. 4:12-16; 2 Tim. 2:4; 4:1-5; Acts 6:2, 4). No man can properly give himself to more than one employment, and no man can devote himself to the work of the ministry if he is obliged to give his attention to earthly concerns. It is not so much the time involved as it is the care of other concerns which forbids gospel preachers from engaging in secular, material, worldly concerns. In so far as it is possible for them to do so, deacons are responsible to relieve their pastor of all mundane care, so that he has no need to concern himself with anything except prayer, study and preaching. They are to see that the material needs of the pastor and his family are supplied by the church. They are to assume care for the church property, making certain that it is properly maintained. They are to see that the needs of widows and orphans in the church family are met, and they are to see that the work of the ministry is not hindered because of any lack of financial, material supplies.

Of course, it must not be assumed that the deacons are personally responsible to meet all these needs, but they are responsible to distribute the funds of the church with prudence and to see that these things are taken care of. They are not 'watchdogs' over the church funds, but they are stewards of the church funds.

2. How were the first deacons chosen?

It seems likely, at least to me, that the church at Jerusalem was made up of several congregations, which met in several places throughout the city to worship God. When Luke tells us that the apostles 'called the multitude of the disciples unto them', I doubt that he means us to understand that all the thousands of disciples came together. Probably, as Matthew Henry suggests, they called the heads of the various congregations together to select the deacons.

The apostles, acting under the influence of the Holy Spirit, called the preachers from the various congregations together and told them to choose out of their congregations seven men who would collectively serve the tables of the poor. This, in my opinion, is a reasonable conjecture from the information given in the book of Acts. Many will certainly take exception to this view, but I think this is what happened. Be that as it may, we know these three things about the selection of these seven men.

1. *They were chosen in compliance with the apostles' instructions.* These deacons were not chosen by the whim and fancy of the congregation, but by the direction of those men responsible for the oversight of the church.

2. *They were chosen from among the men of the church.* Deacons are not selected from one local church and brought to another; they are selected from among the people they serve. Those chosen to fill the deacon's office are to be men, not women. No doubt some will charge those who adhere to God's Word in this matter with sexism and bigotry, but the Word of God never gives women any position of authority or rule, either in the home or in the church.

3. *They were ordained by the apostles.* The apostles were God's representatives and God's ordained messengers to his church. They alone were responsible for the oversight of the church, and they alone had the prerogative of ordaining, or not ordaining, men to the

deacon's office. Today, that responsibility falls upon the shoulders of the pastor and elders of a congregation.

3. What kind of men may be ordained to the office of deacon?

The Word of God clearly describes the character of those men who might properly be ordained to the office of a deacon. Deacons must never be chosen on the basis of friendship, but on the basis of faithfulness.

In Acts 6:3 the Holy Spirit gives us three characteristics of those men who might be selected to serve as deacons in God's house.

1. *A deacon must be a man of 'honest report'.* He must be a man of honesty, integrity, dependability and good reputation. Both in the church and in the community at large, the deacon must be respected as a man of principle and moral integrity.

2. *A deacon must be a man 'full of the Holy Ghost'.* That simply means, he must be a man whose life is controlled by God the Holy Spirit (Eph. 5:18). No man should ever be ordained to the office of a deacon whose daily life, conduct, speech and attitude are contrary to the grace and fruit of God the Holy Spirit (Gal. 5:22-23). The deacon must be a man who is led by the Spirit, whose life is evidently under the dominion of the Spirit.

3. *He must be a man who possesses 'wisdom'.* It is not necessary that a deacon be well educated, but it is necessary for him to be wise. Mature judgement is essential.

In 1 Timothy 3:8-12 Paul gives eight additional characteristics which must be found in those men who might be selected to serve as deacons in the church of God.

4. *Deacons must be 'grave'.* 'Grave' does not mean long-faced, sour, or unhappy! It means 'sober-minded'. Only those who take serious things seriously can serve as deacons.

5. *Deacons must not be 'doubletongued'.* They must be honest men whose word can be depended upon, whose confidence can be trusted. Men who are prone to gossip must never be given the office of a deacon.

6. *They must not be 'given to much wine'*. A deacon must be a man of temperance and sobriety, avoiding any lack of moderation, especially drunkenness. This is not a prohibition against the use of alcoholic beverages; it is a prohibition against drunkenness.

7. *A deacon must not be 'greedy of filthy lucre'*. Any man who possesses an inordinate desire for wealth cannot be trusted with the financial concerns of the church, and must not be placed in the deacon's office.

8. *Deacons must be men who hold 'the mystery of the faith in a pure conscience'*. Though deacons are not necessarily gifted as teachers, they must be thoroughly convinced of gospel truth. They must understand and believe the gospel of God's free and sovereign grace in Christ.

9. *They must 'first be proved'*. No novice can ever be appointed to any office in the church. Faithfulness must first be proved in the everyday affairs of life. A man who is not faithful before being ordained as a deacon will not become faithful after he is ordained.

10. *Their wives also must be 'faithful in all things'*. Because deacons are trusted with confidential matters, no man should be made a deacon whose wife is a busybody, a gossip, or a slanderer. If a man's wife is not committed to the gospel, he cannot serve well as a deacon.

11. *Every deacon must be the head of his own house.* He must be the husband of one wife. As in the case of elders, Paul is not forbidding the deacon's office to a man who has remarried after his first wife has died, or one who has remarried after having been lawfully divorced. He is guarding the church against the common Gentile practice of polygamy. Nothing more is to be inferred from the statement: 'Let the deacons be the husbands of one wife.'
     He must also rule his household in the fear of God. If a man does not exercise his God-given responsibilities in his home, he cannot be given the greater responsibility of the deacon's office.
     These eleven characteristics are not suggestions to us about what deacons should be ideally. These are essential qualifications which must be found in any man who is given the privilege and

responsibility of the deacon's office. Those who ignore these requirements insult God, and they will suffer the consequences of their actions.

4. What is the work for which deacons are ordained?

The word 'deacon' simply means 'servant'. A deacon is a man who serves the church of Christ, the interests of the gospel and the pastor who preaches the gospel to him. As the first deacons were chosen to relieve the apostles of the burden of caring for the poor, so it is the work of deacons to do anything and everything they can to relieve their pastor of any burden or care that would take his time and attention away from the preaching of the gospel. Deacons are to set and serve the Lord's Table. They are to take care of the physical and monetary concerns of the church. They are to visit the sick and relieve the poor of the congregation. Deacons are to see that their pastor has no worldly concern to distract him from, or interfere with, the work of the gospel ministry. The primary purpose for the office of a deacon is that God's servant may give himself continually, without distraction or interruption, to prayer, study and preaching (Acts 6:2,4). What could be more noble, beneficial to the souls of men, or honouring to a man?

5. What effect did the service of the first seven deacons have on the church at Jerusalem and the ministry of the gospel?

Let no deacon take his work lightly. Let no pastor or church member look upon the work of faithful deacons with anything less than the highest esteem. Faithful deacons were a real asset to the early church. As a result of their faithful service, we read, 'And the word of God increased; and the number of the disciples multiplied in Jerusalem greatly; and a great company of the priests were obedient to the faith' (Acts 6:7). Because seven men were willing to serve tables a great multitude of elect, redeemed sinners heard the gospel and were called to the obedience of faith by the irresistible grace and power of God the Holy Spirit. Such men, such faithful deacons, wherever they are found, are a great asset to God's servants and his church.

Because of the quiet, unassuming service of seven faithful deacons, the Holy Spirit tells us that two things happened.

1. *The Word of God increased.* The gospel was preached more fully and more freely to more people than could have been possible without the service of those first deacons.

2. *The church grew greatly.* Many were converted because God's servants were free to exercise their gifts in preaching the gospel. Many, who otherwise could not have been reached by the gospel, heard the Word and believed because seven faithful men served as deacons in the church at Jerusalem.

Let the names of these seven men, and all who faithfully serve the office of a deacon, be written in gold: Stephen, Philip, Prochorus, Nicanor, Timon, Parmenas and Nicolas. By their service many heard and believed the gospel preached by the apostles. By the services of their successors many more will hear and believe the gospel of the grace of God. Those men who serve faithfully as deacons earn and deserve the respect and esteem of the pastors and churches they serve (1 Tim. 3:13).

Faithful deacons are rare, but they are a great blessing to the pastors and churches they serve. How I thank God for the faithful deacons he has given me! Only eternity will reveal the worth of those men who faithfully take care of the earthly, material concerns of the church so that God's servants might freely preach the gospel of Christ.

I call upon all who have the office of a deacon to use it well, as those first seven deacons did. Serve the church of God like the Levites served the nation of Israel. Serve your pastor like Aaron and Hur served Moses. Minister to the needs of God's church, and hold up the hands of God's servant, your pastor, in the work of the gospel, for the honour of Christ and the increase of his kingdom.

9.
Three gospel ordinances

'Then they that gladly received his word were baptized: and the same day there were added unto them about three thousand souls. And they continued steadfastly in the apostles' doctrine and fellowship, and in breaking of bread, and in prayers. And fear came upon every soul: and many wonders and signs were done by the apostles. And all that believed were together, and had all things common; and sold their possessions and goods, and parted them to all men, as every man had need. And they, continuing daily with one accord in the temple, and breaking bread from house to house, did eat their meat with gladness and singleness of heart, praising God, and having favour with all the people. And the Lord added to the church daily such as should be saved' (Acts 2:41-47).

On the Day of Pentecost the apostle Peter preached the gospel to a great multitude. He simply told them the wondrous story of redemption accomplished and grace performed by Christ, and proclaimed the fact of Christ's glorious exaltation and dominion as Lord and King of the universe. He preached with the power of the Holy Spirit upon him. When he had finished, 3,000 men and women had been converted by the grace of God. They were all baptized and added to the church in one day! The text which heads this chapter shows us three things which characterized these early believers, three things which were tokens of God's grace upon his people at Jerusalem.

1. *Baptism*. 'They that gladly received his word were baptized.'

2. *Church membership.* 'There were added unto them [the church] about three thousand souls.'

3. *The Lord's Supper.* 'And they continued steadfastly in the apostles' doctrine and fellowship, and in breaking of bread, and in prayers.'

In this and the following chapters we shall examine what the Word of God has to say about our responsibilities as believers to these three gospel ordinances. These three things should be of great interest and concern to every believer. They are matters about which every local church needs to be well informed and firmly established.

As we saw in chapter 2, the church of God is made up of all true believers in every age. God's elect are his church. Some are in heaven, and some are on earth; but all true believers, in heaven and on earth, are one body in Christ. The Scriptures make this explicitly clear (Matt. 16:18; Eph. 1:22-23; 5:25-27; Heb. 12:22-24).

However, the New Testament places great emphasis upon the local church, the importance of its ministry and every believer's responsibility to it (Matt. 18:20; 28:18-20; 1 Tim. 3:15). Most of the epistles are addressed to local churches. Our Lord's means of accomplishing his work in this world is the ministry of local churches. The Great Commission was given to and is carried out by local churches. Local churches support, maintain and send out pastors and missionaries to preach the gospel. Local churches administer the ordinances of Christ. The local church is a family, a brotherhood, a body of believers united together in Christ (1 Cor. 12:25-27). Every local church should be a miniature of the church universal (Eph. 2:20-22; 4:1-7).

Our relationship to the church of Christ is a matter of obedience to Christ our Lord. It is a great privilege for any man or woman to be a part of a true gospel church. But with that privilege there is a great responsibility. Every believer needs to understand clearly his responsibilities to the local church. Our relationship with the church of Christ, in great measure, reveals our relationship with Christ. The attitude we have about our responsibilities to the local church is only a reflection of our attitude towards Christ, who is the Head of the church.

In this chapter I will give a brief definition of baptism, church membership and the Lord's Supper. We shall then study each of these ordinances in much more detail in the four following chapters.

1. Baptism

Baptism is the believer's public confession of faith in Christ. It is not meritorious. It has no saving efficacy. It cannot regenerate, wash away sin, or even sanctify. It is a confession of faith, no more and no less.

Baptism is a symbolic picture of the gospel. Ananias said to Saul, after he had seen the Lord, heard his voice and believed, 'Arise, and be baptized, and wash away thy sins, calling on the name of the Lord' (Acts 22:16). Obviously, he did not mean that the waters of baptism could wash away sin! Only the blood of Christ can do that. He put away all the sins of God's elect, which were imputed to him when he died as our substitute (Heb. 9:26). But baptism is a picture of our sins being washed away by our Saviour's blood. We are buried with Christ, symbolically, in baptism, because we died with him and were buried with him when he bore the wrath of God as our substitute. Baptism has nothing to do with the accomplishment of salvation, but it is a symbolic figure of salvation's accomplishment by the death, burial and resurrection of Christ, the sinner's substitute (1 Peter 3:21).

Baptism is the believer's public identification with Christ and his people in this world. When God saves one of his elect, the one who has been saved separates himself from unsaved family and friends by his baptism. His baptism says, 'I was lost and blind, groping about in the darkness of false religion. But now God has saved me by his free grace in Christ. And I want all to know that this sovereign Christ is my Saviour and Lord and his people are my people.'

Baptism is the believer's public avowal of commitment to Christ as Lord and the glory of his great name. As we have been raised together with Christ representatively (Eph. 2:5-6) and raised from spiritual death to spiritual life in Christ by the power of his grace (John 5:25), we rise up out of the waters of baptism declaring to all the world that we will henceforth walk with our Lord in the newness of life (Rom. 6:4).

Many reasons might be given why all believers should be baptized, but for the sake of brevity I will simply give here three reasons for our baptism. Firstly, our Lord did it (Mark 1:9-11). Secondly, our Lord commands it (Mark 16:15-16). Thirdly, every believer's conscience requires it (1 Peter 3:21). We cannot follow Christ's example, obey his Word, or satisfy the requirements of our renewed consciences until we have been immersed in the name of our Lord.

2. Church membership

Church membership is the believer's fellowship and communion with Christ in his body. Many think little of church membership. Many who claim to be believers are not identified with, or committed to, any local church. But in the New Testament men and women who followed Christ, by one means or another, applied for and obtained membership in local churches. They publicly identified themselves with and committed themselves to the church of God. Paul 'assayed to join himself to the disciples' at Jerusalem, and was publicly received by them into the church (Acts 9:26-31). Phoebe was recommended to the fellowship of the church at Rome by the apostle Paul (Rom. 16:1).

Church membership is restricted to believers only. A local church is a body of believers, voluntarily united together in the name of Christ for the glory of Christ, the furtherance of the gospel, the salvation of God's elect and mutual edification.

The fellowship of believers in a local church is vital to their spiritual welfare. Our individual spiritual growth in the grace and knowledge of our Lord Jesus Christ is in many ways dependent upon our relationship to and fellowship with the body of Christ. Believers need the fellowship of other believers. We all need encouragement from others. We need the strength of our brethren. We need one another.

Some years ago, a wise old pastor went to visit a member of his congregation who had been neglecting the worship of God, with the hope of encouraging his erring brother to be steadfast in the faith. As the two men sat by the hearth chatting, the pastor raked out one of the red-hot coals. That coal, lying by itself, apart from the other burning coals, soon grew cold. The pastor picked it up in his hand

and held it out to his friend, saying, 'One coal by itself cannot burn very long. It needs the heat of many, or its fire will die.' The neglectful man, with a tear in his eye, said, 'I get the message. Thank you. I will be in my place next Sunday.' And he was. Church membership is vital. You and I simply cannot exist without the ministry of the Word and the fellowship of God's saints in worship. Basically, membership in a local church involves three things.

1. Church membership is an openly avowed, public commitment to the body of Christ (Phil. 2:1-4). It is like a marriage ceremony. Without inward commitment the ceremony is nothing. But for a woman to move in with a man who will not make a public commitment to her is an act of desperation, or folly, or both.

If we are committed to the family of believers to which we belong, we enjoy their company, pray for their spiritual well-being, give to meet the needs of the family, serve the family's interest, speak well of the family members and promote the family's interest. Let each one of us see that we live up to our professed commitment.

2. Church membership gives us the privilege of communion and fellowship with the body of Christ. 'Behold, how good and how pleasant it is for brethren to dwell together in unity' (Ps. 133:1). The fellowship of God's people in public worship is most delightful and blessed because in the fellowship of God's saints we find fellowship with Christ (Matt. 18:20). Our Saviour still walks in the midst of the golden lampstands and makes himself known in his churches (Rev. 1:12, 13, 20).

Who can estimate the value and privilege of being a member of a local church where Christ is honoured by the unity, peace, fellowship and love of the saints? If God has given us such a privilege, let us jealously guard and promote the unity of the Spirit, the bond of peace and the fellowship of love he has given (Eph. 4:1-7).

Church membership is much more than having your name on a church register. It is commitment to the body of Christ. It is communion with Christ in his body.

3. Church membership is care for the body of Christ (1 Cor. 12:24-27). God's people care for and take care of one another. Within the local church family, believers look out for one another's welfare.

They seek opportunities to help, encourage, comfort and cheer one another. But this kindness, affection and care extends beyond the local assembly. It reaches out to God's saints wherever they are found (Heb. 13:1-3).

3. The Lord's Supper

The Lord's Supper is the believer's blessed remembrance of Christ. One of the greatest, most blessed privileges we have in this world is that of coming together at the Lord's Table to celebrate our redemption in Christ, by eating the bread and drinking the wine in remembrance of our Saviour. The Lord's Supper is not a pompous religious ceremony, shrouded in mystery and performed with pageantry. It is a very simple, but very precious, picture of our redemption by Christ. Every child of God needs to know the meaning and significance of this blessed ordinance, so that he may receive it, enjoy it and profit by it to the fullest possible degree (1 Cor. 11:23-28).

Our Lord Jesus gave us this ordinance as a perpetual symbol and picture to remind us of himself and the work he performed on earth as our representative and substitute (Luke 22:7-20). Knowing that he would be physically absent from his beloved church for some time he left us a picture of himself, to remind us constantly of his great love for us. Each time we break the bread and drink the wine, we show forth the Lord's death (1 Cor. 11:26), proclaiming to ourselves and to all who see the ordinance the redemption of our souls by the death of Christ in our place. Like baptism the Lord's Supper is a picture of the gospel.

The basis of our faith is the Word of God alone. We must add nothing to it and take nothing from it. We must obey every precept of the Word, follow every precedent of the Word and reverently observe every ordinance of the Word. It is our responsibility to obey Christ and keep his ordinances exactly as he gave them. We need never fear doing what our Lord has commanded us to do. Let us all make it our business to obey and rejoice in these three gospel ordinances of baptism, church membership and the Lord's Supper.

10.
The gospel ordinance of baptism

'And he said unto them, Go ye into all the world, and preach the gospel to every creature. He that believeth and is baptized shall be saved; but he that believeth not shall be damned' (Mark 16:15-16).

The gospel ordinance of baptism is of great importance to every believer, because baptism is a commandment of our Lord Jesus Christ to which all true believers conscientiously submit. Many are willing to compromise this ordinance for the sake of what they call 'Christian unity'. We are told, 'After all, baptism is a matter of secondary importance.' This is a mistake. No commandment given by our Lord is of secondary importance. Baptism is not an optional thing, which we may or may not choose to do at our own discretion. Baptism is essential.

I admit that in so far as salvation is concerned, baptism is a secondary matter. Indeed, it is not even secondary: baptism has nothing to do with salvation. But in the matter of a believer's obedience to God, baptism is essential. It is the answer of a good conscience towards God. Therefore it must be conscientiously observed. Baptism is the outward profession of what we have experienced in our hearts. It is the outward symbol of an inward reality. Therefore it must not be taken lightly.

1. A basic principle

Here is a basic, essential principle of biblical interpretation: when we want to understand what the Word of God teaches about any specific subject or doctrine, we must go to that place in the Bible where that subject or doctrine is taught and explained. Believers' baptism is explained in Romans 6:1-11. If we study that passage carefully, interpreting all other statements about baptism by it, we shall understand what the Word of God teaches about baptism.

2. Errors about baptism

Errors concerning baptism come from two extremes. They either add to what the Scriptures teach, making baptism more than it is, or they take away from what the Scriptures teach, making baptism less than it is. Here are four common errors about baptism.

Sacramentalism

The Catholic church and many Protestant denominations make baptism to be a sacrament, a means of grace. The Bible nowhere suggests that baptism confers grace upon a person. Men and women are not regenerated, born again, or sealed into the covenant of grace by baptism — and neither are infants.

The practice of infant baptism is a remnant of Catholicism among Protestants. There is no basis for it in the Word of God. The practice is nowhere commanded and there is no example of it. It is altogether of human invention. The practice of baptizing babies arose from the heretical notion that baptism has some saving merit and efficacy.

Landmarkism

Landmark Baptists make baptism a basis for a believer's rank, position and reward in heaven. Though they try to deny it, they too make baptism a sacrament. Landmarkers contend that no one has valid New Testament baptism who has not been baptized by the authority of a Landmark church, and that those who are not members of Landmark churches will be, at best, second-class citizens in heaven!

The validity of baptism does not depend upon the credibility of the one who is baptizing, but upon the heart attitude of the one being baptized. Nowhere in the New Testament do we read of anyone who had been baptized as a believer ever being rebaptized. Anyone who reads the Bible, without bias, must recognize that the idea of baptism being a basis of reward in heaven is utterly blasphemous. Salvation is not by works, but by grace alone. Heaven is not the reward of our baptism, but the reward of our Saviour's obedience.

Ritualism

Many observe the ordinance of baptism as an empty, meaningless ritual of religious ceremony, without faith in Christ and without any knowledge of what the ordinance represents.

No one should ever be baptized without an understanding of what he or she is doing. Baptism involves commitment. It symbolizes the gospel. It is a profession of faith in Christ. Those who do not, or cannot, understand the meaning of the ordinance should not be baptized. For this reason, I strongly discourage the practice of baptizing young children. Those who are too young and immature to govern their own lives should never be baptized.

Dispensationalism

Many today would have us believe that baptism is not necessary at all, that it is not an ordinance of the New Testament. To such people I would say, 'Read the book of Acts.' But their response to that is, 'The book of Acts is not a New Testament book'! I might then say, 'Read Romans 6.' But they would say, 'Romans 6 is not talking about water baptism.' They will go to any extreme to defend their system of doctrine and avoid the claims of God's Word upon them.

Enough said about erroneous views of baptism. What is the doctrine of the New Testament regarding this blessed ordinance of the gospel? I want to show that the Lord Jesus Christ commands every believer to follow him in baptism, as a matter of conscientious obedience to him, as a symbolic confession of faith in him. In the following paragraphs we will raise six questions about the gospel ordinance of baptism and seek to answer them from the Word of God.

1. Who should be baptized?

This is a point of great controversy. Throughout our history Baptists have insisted that baptism is to be administered to men and women only upon their profession of personal faith in the Lord Jesus Christ. We insist that faith is the necessary prerequisite to baptism. But is this practice of requiring faith before baptism scriptural? Is it in accordance with the New Testament? Our concern must be not what Baptists believe, or what Protestants believe, but only this — what does the Word of God teach? If we insist upon anything as a matter of religious observance, we must have some definite precept or precedent for it.

There is not one example of infant baptism, or even the baptism of children, in all the New Testament. Everywhere in the New Testament baptism was administered only to those who showed personal repentance towards, and faith in, the Lord Jesus Christ (Matt. 3:7-8; Acts 2:38, 41; 8:37; 19:4-5). Only those who believe on the Lord Jesus Christ may be baptized 'for [because of] the remission of sins' accomplished by Christ and received by faith.

If you believe on Christ, you not only may be baptized, you must. If you do not believe, you cannot be baptized. Faith is the one prerequisite to this ordinance. It is just as dangerous to your soul to be baptized without faith in Christ as it is to eat the bread and drink the wine at the Lord's Supper without faith. To all who desire baptism, the requirement of the New Testament is, 'If thou believest with all thine heart, thou mayest' (Acts 8:37).

You must *believe on the Lord Jesus Christ* (John 1:12-13). Salvation is received by faith alone. But that faith is a personal thing. No sponsor, representative, or 'godparent' can believe for another person, infant or adult. If the Lord Jesus Christ is the only pillar of your hope, the only stay of your soul, the only confidence of your heart, if he is all your righteousness and all your redemption, then God says to you, 'Arise and be baptized' (Acts 22:16). But if you do not yourself trust Christ, the waters of baptism are forbidden to you. Everything in God's house is given to those who believe.

When I speak of faith in Christ, I do not mean that you must give a mere mental assent to the truth of the gospel. You must *believe with all your heart*. Christ must be loved as well as trusted. He must be obeyed as well as believed. Heart faith reverences Christ, worships Christ, submits to Christ, trusts Christ and loves Christ, preferring him above all others. Do you, with your heart's affection and commitment, trust the Lord Jesus Christ? If you do, then you are to be baptized. Baptism is a privilege and responsibility given to all believers, but only to believers.

2. What must a person believe in order to be baptized?

It is not enough simply to have faith. Faith must arise from a sense of personal need and must be fixed upon the proper object. I do not mean to suggest that a person must be a theologian to be saved. But I am saying that a person must be instructed in and knowledgeable of the person and work of Christ to exercise saving faith in Christ. Someone may be ignorant of many things, and yet have faith. But no one can be ignorant of Christ and the gospel of his grace and yet have faith.

Take the example of the Ethiopian eunuch (Acts 8:32-38). Philip preached the gospel to that man, as it is revealed in Isaiah 53:7-8, and the eunuch believed the message Philip delivered. He believed God's message concerning his own sin, acknowledging his own guilt, depravity and just condemnation (Isa. 53:6). He believed God's message regarding the incarnation, obedience and substitutionary sacrifice of Christ. He not only believed that Christ died in the place of God's elect, but that he both satisfied divine justice and put away our sins by his death, securing the eternal salvation of those for whom he died (Isa. 53:5, 10, 11). The Ethiopian eunuch also believed God's testimony regarding the resurrection, ascension, exaltation and intercession of Christ (Isa. 53:10-12). He believed that Jesus is the Christ, the Son of the living God, and that he has the power to save helpless sinners. The point I am making is this: gospel knowledge is necessary to saving faith and to believer's baptism (Romans 10:13-17). As Philip required faith in the Ethiopian eunuch before he would baptize him, so God's servants today must require faith in Christ as a prerequisite to baptism. If a man will not believe, he cannot be baptized. 'He that believeth and is baptized shall be saved; but he that believeth not shall be damned' (Mark 16:16).

3. How is baptism to be performed?

If men were not prejudiced by human opinion and religious tradition this question would be redundant. Baptism can only be performed by immersion. Immersion is not a mode of baptism: immersion is baptism. Baptism is a burial in water, symbolic of death, our death to the law in the person of Christ our substitute (Rom. 6:3-4; Col.

2:12). To substitute sprinkling with water, or pouring water on the head, for burial in water is to imply that atonement is not necessary to salvation and that a man might be accepted before God by mere change of life.

The only means of baptism in the New Testament was immersion. When our Lord Jesus Christ was baptized by John the Baptist he came 'up straightway out of the water' (Matt. 3:16). When the eunuch was baptized by Philip, he 'came up out of the water' (Acts 8:39). They could not have come up out of the water unless they had gone down into the water! In the New Testament much water was required for the ordinance of baptism. A cupful would never do. Men cannot very well go down into and come up out of the water contained in a 'baptismal font'!

Baptism is a burial in water (Rom. 6:4; Col. 2:12). Until a corpse can be buried by sprinkling a few grains of sand in the face and pouring a cup of dirt on the head, a man cannot be baptized by sprinkling or pouring a little water on him. Baptism represents the believer's redemption by the death of Christ as our substitute, and death requires a burial. Those who value the Word of God and understand the meaning of this ordinance realize that the method of baptism is important.

4. When should a believer be baptized?

Many today require a waiting period between a sinner's conversion and his baptism. It is to be a time of proving, examination and instruction. Many reasons are given for this practice. But where is the foundation for it in the Word of God? In the New Testament baptism was never postponed, even for a short time. As soon as a man believes he is to be baptized.

The fact that baptism in the apostolic age was always administered to those who were converted on the day they professed faith in Christ makes it evident that none were recognized as believers who were not instructed in the gospel of Christ. While we must oppose the easy-believism and decisionism of our day, which calls for men and women to trust an unknown, unrevealed Christ, we must not alter the ordinance of Christ. There will always be apostates and false professors in the church. Satan always sows tares where God plants wheat, but it is not our responsibility to separate the tares from the wheat. That is God's work (Matt. 13:24-30). Because man always judges by sight when he tries to separate the tares from the wheat, he pulls up the wheat and keeps the tares. Only God can separate the two, for only he looks at the heart.

5. Why must every believer be baptized?

If baptism is urgently pressed upon God's saints, if it is given such a place of importance as we have seen, there must be good reasons for us to observe it faithfully.

Every believer should be baptized, because *baptism is the believer's first act of obedience to King Jesus*. It is the answer of a good conscience towards God. Knowing that baptism is the ordinance of our Lord, we submit to it as such. In doing so, we discharge a good conscience and have joy and peace (1 Peter 3:21; Matt. 28:18). Obedience to that which we know to be the will of our God gives us peace; and it is impossible for a believer to have the peace of obedience until he follows his Lord in baptism.

Baptism is the believer's public identification with the despised people of God in this world. It is a public renunciation of the world, its religion and our former way of life in it. It is an acknowledgement that we have become the children of God by his free grace. Baptism is the line of separation between the church and the world. When men and women were converted from Judaism, or from Gentile paganism, they renounced their former religion as a damning delusion, identified themselves with Christ, the gospel of his free and sovereign grace, and his despised people in this world, by their baptism. The Ethiopian eunuch, by his baptism, renounced his former religion, Judaism, as an apostate, godless and damning religion. And we, by our baptism, renounce the free-will, works religion of this world, as apostate, godless and damning, saying to all men, 'Christ is the way!'

Primarily, *baptism is the believer's public profession of faith in Christ.* It is a symbolic confession of the gospel of our Lord Jesus Christ. In baptism we confess our union with Christ and our confidence in him as our representative before God (Gal. 3:27). Being buried with Christ symbolically in the waters of baptism, we acknowledge our sin and its just punishment, and we testify of our faith in Christ's substitutionary death for the satisfaction of justice by which our sins have been put away (Rom. 6:3). Rising up from the watery grave, we confess our faith in the resurrection of Christ, our representative resurrection in Christ, our spiritual resurrection by Christ and our bodily resurrection in the likeness of Christ (Rom. 6:4; Col. 2:12). Being raised up from spiritual death by the grace of God in regeneration, through the merits of Christ's obedience, we confess to God and all the world that we will henceforth 'walk in the newness of life', for the glory of our God.

I am often asked, 'Can a person be saved without baptism?' The answer is obvious. Of course! All of God's people are saved without baptism. Salvation is by grace alone (Eph. 2:8-9). But refusal to be baptized is rebellion against the plain command of God. In the New Testament all who were received as brethren and regarded as believers were those who had been baptized. I cannot find one person regarded as a believer in the New Testament who refused baptism.

Another question which is sometimes asked is: 'Should believers ever be rebaptized?' If someone has been baptized since he believed the gospel, there is no reason for him ever to be baptized again. To do so would be a mockery of the ordinance. However, if someone was immersed before God saved him, in some profession of false religion, then that person needs to be baptized and confess Christ.

6. What is expected of those men and women who are baptized?

It is expected that every believer should walk in the newness of life which he or she has professed in baptism. After instructing us in the meaning of baptism and the believer's complete justification by the obedience of Christ, the apostle Paul urges us to look upon our lives as God looks upon us in Christ: 'Likewise also reckon ye also yourselves to be dead indeed unto sin, but alive unto God through Jesus Christ our Lord' (Rom. 6:11).

The man or woman who has been baptized in the name of Christ is expected to be faithful to the gospel, dedicated to the people of

God and committed to the glory of God. We have an example of this new way of life into which every believer, by his or her baptism, professes to enter in Acts 2:41-47. In those early days, they that gladly received the Word of God were baptized and these seven things characterized their lives.

1. *They addicted themselves to the doctrine of the gospel, the fellowship of the saints, the worship of Christ and the joyous exercise of prayer* (v.42). They would not receive any doctrine but the doctrine of Christ crucified. They were united in heart to one another in Christ. They allowed nothing to keep them from the fellowship of the saints and the ordinances of public worship.

2. *They had all things in common* (v. 44). Because they had Christ in common and grace in common, they had all their gifts, talents and worldly goods in common. This text does not suggest communal living in separation from unbelieving men. We cannot serve the interests of Christ's kingdom and the souls of men, or even our own souls' welfare, by isolating ourselves from the world. We are to live among men for the glory of God (Titus 2:10-14). However, we are to look upon our earthly goods as the public property of God's church, to be used and dispensed by us for the furtherance of the gospel and the good of our brethren.

3. *They displayed great unity of spirit, being all of one accord* (v. 46). The men and women of that early church had one thing that brought them together and kept them together — the love of Christ. They loved Christ, loved the gospel of his grace and loved one another for Christ's sake. They willingly put aside petty grievances and personal ambition for the greater cause of Christ's glory in all things.

4. *They served God and one another with 'singleness of heart'* (v. 46). Their hearts were sincere. And with sincerity they set their hearts upon one great object, which took precedence over all other things. Above all things and in all things those early believers sought the glory of Christ.

5. *Their hearts were full of praise towards God* (v. 47). They could

not get over the wonder of redemption. They praised God the Father
for his electing love, God the Son for his blood atonement and God
the Spirit for his effectual call. Personally and collectively the
members of that early church were astonished at God's great grace
upon them in Christ.

You can be sure of this: any congregation of saved sinners,
astonished by God's grace towards them in Christ, loving Christ and
sincerely seeking his glory will be of 'one accord'.

6. *These men and women lived blamelessly, above reproach, in their
conduct before the world* (v. 47). They were by no means perfect.
But they were honest, thrifty, hard-working men and women. They
paid their bills, gave an honest day's work for an honest day's pay,
and refrained from the gossip and slander of men and from murmuring and complaining against God. Though men hated their
doctrine, they could not legitimately charge them with evil. They
walked as men who walked with God!

7. *'And the Lord added to the church daily such as should be saved'*
(v. 47). It is written, 'Them that honour me, I will honour.' And as
these early believers lived consistently with what they professed in
their baptism they were honoured by God. God used them for the
salvation of his elect. Those who were added to the church were
added by the work of the Lord. Those who were saved were 'such
as should be saved', those whom God elected in eternity and Christ
purchased at Calvary. And the Lord added to his church daily! May
he be pleased to make his church in these days a people known by
such gracious characteristics for the honour of his name! And may
it please our Lord again to add to the church daily such as should be
saved!

Do you believe on the Lord Jesus Christ? If you do and have not
yet been baptized, I urge you to confess him in baptism. Enlist
beneath the blood-stained banner of the cross with all the redeemed.
Renounce your life of rebellion. Repent of your dead works of
religion and self-righteousness. Confess Christ as your Lord and
Saviour publicly, in the way he has prescribed, by believer's
baptism. Secret disciples, like Nicodemus and Joseph of
Arimathæa, must always be suspect disciples.

Have you already confessed Christ in baptism as a believer? If
you have, I urge you to live according to your profession. We are

crucified with Christ. Let us, therefore, count this world to be a dead thing. We are risen with Christ. Let us, therefore, walk in the newness of life (Col. 3:1-3). Here is the basis of my appeal: 'Ye are not your own. For ye are bought with a price: therefore glorify God in your body, and in your spirit, which are God's' (1 Cor. 6:20).

11.
Church membership

'And the multitude of them that believed were of one heart and of one soul: neither said any of them that ought of the things which he possessed was his own; but they had all things common. And with great power gave the apostles witness of the resurrection of the Lord Jesus: and great grace was upon them all' (Acts 4:32-33).

These two verses describe the essence of what church membership should be. Every local church should seek to mould itself after the pattern of the New Testament. And here the Holy Spirit gives us an example of church membership at its best. He tells us five things about the church at Jerusalem, which I want us to examine as an example of what every local church should be.

1. *The members of this first church were believers.* I do not suggest, or imply, that they were all true believers. Ananias and Sapphira demonstrate clearly that, even in this church, tares always grow with the wheat. The visible church, from the beginning, has been a mixed multitude. We must not be surprised to see men and women in our own congregations prove themselves to be reprobate and not re-generate. But all the members of this early church professed to be believers. They all professed faith in and allegiance to the Lord Jesus Christ by public baptism (Acts 2:41).

2. *This local church was a body of believers united as one in Christ.*

They 'were of one heart and of one soul'. They were truly united as one body in Christ. This was not a divided congregation. Because they were united to one Head, they were one body. Because they were ruled by one King, they were a united kingdom. Because they were born of one Spirit, they were one family. Peace was a reality in this local church, because the Prince of Peace ruled in their hearts. They were one in Christ! In heart, in spirit, in doctrine and in purpose, these men and women were one in Christ. Grace had made them one.

3. *The members of this first New Testament church were devoted to each other.* 'Neither said any of them that ought of the things which he possessed was his own, but they had all things common.' God's people own nothing. What we have, we have as stewards of God, for the service of his kingdom. If we do not use what God has put in our hands for the good of his kingdom, but take it for our own pleasure and gratification, we rob God! In those early days of the church God's people took care of each other — and they still do!

4. *This local church was committed to the preaching of the gospel.* It appears that this young congregation was supporting at least twelve regular preachers and their families (1 Cor. 9:5). They provided the needs of all eleven apostles and Matthias. They fed, clothed, housed and provided all the needs of their preachers and their preachers' wives and children, so that those who were called of God to do so might give themselves exclusively to the work of preaching the gospel. 'And with great power gave the apostles witness of the resurrection of the Lord Jesus.'

The church at Jerusalem knew its responsibility and met it. The Lord Jesus had left them upon the earth for only one purpose, with only one work to do. And they did their work; they fulfilled their purpose: they preached the gospel! The men and women of the church worked hard and gave generously, so that the good news of God's free and sovereign grace in Christ might be freely preached to all.

5. *The source and cause of their faith, unity, devotion to one another and commitment to the preaching of the gospel was the grace of God.* 'Great grace was upon them all.' The things I have described are not natural to men. They are the products of divine grace. Any

church possessing these characteristics is a richly blessed assembly. It owes an infinite debt of gratitude and praise to God for his great grace, so freely bestowed upon undeserving sinners for Christ's sake.

Using the example of the church at Jerusalem as our pattern, I want to show from the Word of God what membership in a local church involves.

A local church is a congregation of redeemed sinners, voluntarily united and committed to one another and to Christ, by their public profession of faith in believers' baptism, for the worship of God through the preaching of the gospel, the observance of his ordinances and the celebration of his praise, for the furtherance of the gospel and the glory of the triune God in this world.

Here are four things plainly revealed in the New Testament about membership in a local church.

1. A local church is a congregation of redeemed sinners

All the members of a local church must be, at least in profession, regenerate men and women, people who are born again by the grace of God, those who believe the gospel. We raise our children under the sound of the gospel. We train them up in the nurture and admonition of the Lord. But children are not raised in the church. Church membership is not a family affair. All who enter into the kingdom of God must be born into it personally by the Spirit of God (John 3:5, 7).

The local church is the family of the redeemed. We have been redeemed by the blood of Christ from the penalty of sin and the curse of the law (Gal. 3:13). And we have been redeemed from the reigning power, guilt and dominion of sin by the power and grace of God the Holy Spirit, who effectually applies the blood of Christ to the hearts of God's elect, producing life and faith in us (Eph. 1:18-20; 2:1-8; Heb. 9:14).

If you are redeemed by the blood of Christ and the grace of God in Christ, you should, like Saul of Tarsus (Acts 9:26), seek membership in a local church where Christ is worshipped and preached in all the fulness of his mediatorial glory. If you have not experienced the grace of God in regeneration, if you have no faith in the

Lord Jesus Christ, you cannot unite with the church of Christ until you are born of God.

We must insist upon a regenerate church membership because the New Testament requires it. The first church was composed only of those who professed faith in Christ by public baptism (Acts 2:41-42). All the letters written to the churches in the New Testament were addressed to those men and women who were called to be saints and brethren in Christ (Rom. 1:6; 1 Cor. 1:2; 2 Cor. 1:1; Gal. 1:2; Eph. 1:1; Phil. 1:1; Col. 1:2; 1 Thess. 1:1-3; 2 Thess. 1:1-3). To allow men, women and children the privilege of church membership without a personal experience of grace is to promote in them a false hope of acceptance with God.

Yet *all the members of God's church in this world, though redeemed by blood and saved by grace, are sinners still.* We make no pretence of perfection in ourselves. We claim no holiness of our own. Our only righteousness is the righteousness of Christ. Our only holiness is that which God has given to us by virtue of our union with Christ.

We are all sinners. We are all apt to err. We are all in need of constant mercy. We are all in need of forgiveness, both by God and one another. Let us therefore be kind, tender, merciful and forgiving towards one another (Eph. 4:32).

There are no perfect churches in this world. God's family is a family of saved sinners who are sympathetic with, and merciful towards, other sinners, for Christ's sake.

2. Membership in a local church is a voluntary union with and commitment to Christ and his people

Church membership is *voluntary.* I cannot find a single example of churches or preachers in the New Testament recruiting members, asking men and women to join the church, or in any way pressuring people to unite with them. We simply preach the gospel to sinners and wait upon God to apply it effectually to their hearts. When he does, he will add them to the church.

When men and women are converted by the grace of God and voluntarily unite and identify with the people of God, their hearts are truly knit together. And when God unites people, they are united. Nothing can separate them.

Church membership is a voluntary *commitment* to the Lord
Jesus and his people. Commitment cannot be forced, or constrained.
It must be voluntary. Rules, covenants and pledges are not needed
when men and women voluntarily commit themselves to Christ and
his people. Grace, gratitude and love make those things useless.

3. The door of entrance into the local church is believers' baptism

Many object to this. They tell us that insistence upon believers'
baptism is sectarian, bigoted and divisive. They urge that we should
leave it to every man's conscience whether he will or will not be
baptized. But the teachings of the New Testament are plain.

Baptism is the believer's first act of obedience to Christ as Lord. In
the book of Acts believers were baptized after they received the
Word in faith and before they were united with the church (Acts
2:41; 8:12).

*All who were recognized in the New Testament as believers and
brethren in Christ were baptized.* The only exception to this is the
penitent thief, who died before he could follow his Lord's command. But his example no more nullifies the necessity of baptism
than it might the necessity of public worship. He never had the
opportunity to engage in either. The fact is, the Word of God gives
us no basis for looking upon anyone as a believer who wilfully
refuses to follow the Lord in baptism (Rom. 6:1-14; Gal. 3:27; 1
Peter 3:21); and if we cannot look upon such people as believers, we
cannot receive them into the membership of the local church.

4. Membership in a local church involves voluntary personal obligation and commitment

When men and women, without force or constraint, voluntarily
unite with the family of God, they place themselves under personal
obligation and responsibility to the local church of which they have
become members (Rom. 12-14; 1 Cor. 12:1-31). When our Saviour
became our surety in the covenant of grace, he voluntarily assumed

all responsibility for the eternal welfare of God's elect. When a man marries a woman, he voluntarily assumes all the obligations and responsibilities of a husband. When believers unite with a local church they make a public commitment to it.

The church of God is my family, and I am committed to my family. I prefer my family to myself. I seek the welfare of my family above my own welfare. I seek the happiness of my family above my own happiness, and I seek the comfort of my family above my own comfort.

God's people are a family, and the members of God's family are committed to one another. Regrettably, there appears to be very little commitment in most men and women who profess to be believers. Commitment is dependability, faithfulness and loyalty. It always requires a measure of self-denial and self-sacrifice. It always requires deliberate effort. It is always costly.

In many ways church membership is similar to baptism. For example, though I was baptized long before I moved to Danville, Kentucky, when I joined Grace Baptist Church at Danville, I publicly identified myself with that congregation and its doctrine. I publicly committed myself to that body of believers, saying, 'Thy people shall be my people and thy God my God.' I voluntarily obligated myself to seek and promote all the objects of that assembly. I am now honour bound to fulfil my responsibilities as a member of that congregation. Basically, I have made myself responsible for five things. These are things for which every member of a local church is responsible.

1. *It is the responsibility of every member of God's family to promote and maintain the worship of God.* The primary purpose for which the saints of God gather in the name of Christ is that we may worship him. Everything done in the house of God must be designed to promote the worship of God and the devotion of our hearts to him. And it is the responsibility of every member of the church personally to pursue those objects.

We are not under the law. Therefore we do not compel anyone to pay a tithe. And God's kingdom is not maintained by the arm of the flesh. Therefore we do not call for pledges. But every member is personally responsible to supply the financial needs of the church and its ministry by generously and regularly giving of his or her finances. As we have seen, commitment to anything involves cost, and love for Christ and the gospel of his grace makes God's saints willing to give cheerfully of their means to meet the needs of his kingdom.

Every member of the church is also personally responsible to support the work of the church by prayer, calling upon God to establish, enlarge and use the ministry of the assembly for the glory of Christ. Pray for your pastor, elders, deacons, teachers and missionaries, as they endeavour to lead God's saints, seek the salvation of his elect and serve the interests of his kingdom. Pray for your brethren, especially for the young, the weak and the needy, and pray for yourself, that your own heart may be touched by the ministry of the gospel.

See to it as well that you promote the worship of God by personal attendance at public worship. Do not neglect the assembly of God's saints. Do not merely fit the worship of God into the schedule of your life, but rather arrange the affairs of your life around the worship of God, so that nothing keeps you from the house of God at the appointed times of public worship.

2. *Every member of the local church is personally responsible to do whatever he or she can for the furtherance of the gospel.* Some are called and gifted of God to preach the gospel. They must preach. Others are gifted of God to provide generously for the ministry of the Word. They must give. Others have talents and abilities by which they may serve the servants of God and his people. They must serve. You are responsible to do what you have the ability to do and use what God has put in your hands for the cause of Christ. No one is required, or expected, to do what he has no ability to do. But everyone is expected to do what God has given him or her the ability to do.

3. *Every member of the church is responsible to seek, by every means God has given, the comfort, growth and edification of his or her brothers and sisters in Christ.* God's people care for, support, help and strengthen one another. Family members love each other, and love makes them responsible for one another. We must especially seek to be of benefit to those who need our help. Everybody wants to find a church where they can experience such love. God's people seek an opportunity to bestow love.

4. *It is the responsibility of every member of the body of Christ to live circumspectly in this world.* For the honour of Christ, the honour of the gospel and the honour of your family, the church of God, order your life so that you bring no reproach. Live with integrity, uprightness, charity and patience in every relationship. At home, on the job, in business, in the community, in all things, seek to honour Christ.

5. *It is every member's personal responsibility to seek and promote the glory of God.* Whatever we do, in word or in deed, let us do all for the glory of God. Let us make the glory of God the single object of our lives. If we do, we will serve Christ, his church and the generation in which we live well.

5. The nature of unity in the local church

Real unity, fellowship and communion in a local church is the gift of God the Holy Spirit. Only God can produce it. Men cannot even counterfeit it. It involves five things.

1. *It is a unity of doctrine* (2 John 9). Doctrinal unity is essential to church fellowship. 'How can two walk together, except they be agreed?' And there is no possibility of doctrinal unity unless the doctrine of the church is the doctrine of Christ, the gospel of God's free and sovereign grace to sinners through the merits of Christ's finished work as the sinner's substitute.

2. *It is an agreement of heart.* Fellowship is more than a uniformity of doctrine. It is a union of hearts. It exists only when men and women both believe and love the doctrine of the gospel. Hearts committed to one object are in fellowship with one another.

3. *It is a dedication to the pursuit of one thing — the glory of God in Christ.* Our hearts must be united in the faith of the gospel and motivated by the same desire. Church fellowship cannot be had unless God's saints together seek the glory of God above all else; and if the members each seek God's glory in Christ church fellowship cannot be lost. Our unity is broken when we lose sight of our object, the glory of God.

4. *Unity, fellowship and communion in a church body can only exist where there is a willing submission to one another for Christ's sake* (Eph. 5:18-25). If men and women want peace at home, they yield to one another, willingly, without resentment, and, in the same way, if men and women want peace in the house of God, they must yield to one another, willingly, without resentment, for Christ's sake. If no issue can divide us but the glory of God and the gospel of his grace, then as long as we are united in that which is vital, we cannot be divided.

5. *The fellowship of God's church is a fellowship of real, sincere love* (Eph. 4:32-5:1). Believers love one another, and love both magnifies virtues and hides faults in its object. It is impossible for men and women who love one another to be divided.

'Now therefore ye are no more strangers and foreigners, but fellow-citizens with the saints, and of the household of God; and are built upon the foundation of the apostles and prophets, Jesus Christ himself being the chief corner-stone; in whom all the building fitly framed together groweth unto an holy temple in the Lord: in whom ye also are builded together for an habitation of God through the Spirit' (Eph. 2:19-22).

We have seen from the Scriptures what church membership involves and what every local church should be. Now let each of us answer this question honestly in our own hearts: what kind of church would my church be if every member had exactly the same level of commitment and love that I have?

12.
Church membership:
our responsibilities to one another

'We being many are one bread, and one body: for we are all partakers of that one bread' (1 Cor. 10:17).

Paul's argument for unity in the church is this: when we come together at the Lord's Table the cup of wine which we receive represents the blood of Christ, and the loaf of bread which we break represents the body of Christ. By eating that bread and drinking that wine we not only show forth the death of Christ as our sin-atoning substitute, we also declare that we are one in Christ and one with Christ.

If the members of the local church are all partakers of Christ by faith, then all are one body in Christ, and it is the responsibility of believers, particularly brethren in the same local church, to treat one another as one member of the body treats another, with mutual care, love and esteem.

Church membership is not a mere denominational affiliation. It is much more than a mere uniformity of doctrine. Church membership is a union of believers with one another in Christ, a spiritual union, a union of hearts. Though we are many individuals, many members, serving different uses, being united to one Head, we are one body in Christ. In Christ we are one. We all have the same Father, even the God and Father of our Lord Jesus Christ. We all have been made partakers of the same divine nature, the nature of Christ. We all have the same elder Brother, the Son of God. We are all born of the same Spirit, the Spirit of God. We are all redeemed by the same blood atonement, even the precious blood of Christ. We all live for the same purpose, the glory of God. We all have the same home in heaven and the same eternal inheritance of grace. We are all 'heirs of God and joint-heirs with Christ'.

If we are born again by the Spirit of God, saved by the grace of God, truly the children of God by faith in the Lord Jesus Christ, then we are one body in Christ. Without question, these things are true of all God's saints in the world. The church of God universal is one. But all these things are particularly true of every true local church; and if we are one body in Christ, we have certain responsibilities to one another, responsibilities which are plainly described in the New Testament.

In this chapter we shall look at twelve things for which every member of the church of God is responsible. These twelve responsibilities of believers to one another are vital to the life and usefulness of every local church.

1. Believers are to love one another (Rom. 12:10; 13:8)

Love is a debt we owe to one another. This love is more than a sentimental feeling. It is an affection of the heart that is seen in the actions of a believer's life. Love causes men and women to prefer one another. Love prefers the comfort of its object to its own comfort, the well-being of its object to its own well-being, and the will of its object to its own will.

Love is what our Master teaches us by his own example (John 13:12-15; 1 John 3:16). It is self-denying, self-sacrificing and willingly serves the needs and interests of its object. Love is the law that governs Christ's kingdom (John 13:34; 15:12, 17; 1 John 3:23). The church of God is not ruled by the law of Moses, or by covenants and rules of order. The church of God is ruled and governed by brotherly love. If our lives are motivated and governed by love for Christ and his people, they are well governed. Love is the evidence of life and faith in Christ (John 13:35; 1 John 3:14). Our love for one another demonstrates to the world that we are the disciples of Christ, and proves the reality of our profession of faith. We know our brethren by their love, and our brethren know us by our love.

Our relationship to one another in the body of Christ obliges us to love one another. We are fellow-citizens, members of the same family, members of one another, a brotherhood of believers. The church of God is a fraternity of love. 'Love the brotherhood' (1 Peter 2:17). All our duty to one another is summed up in this one commandment. If we love one another, we will do what is right. Brotherly love makes life in the body of Christ delightful, comfortable and honourable. 'Behold, how good and how pleasant it is for brethren to dwell together in unity!' (Ps. 133:1). Where there is unity, there is love. And where there is love, there is unity.

2. Every member of the local church must endeavour to keep the unity of the Spirit in the bond of peace (Eph. 4:1-7)

The strength of the church is its unity and peace. Many small sticks may be weak and easily broken. Standing alone they are useless. They can be used for nothing but making noise and inflicting pain; but bind them all together as one, and they are unbreakable, mighty and useful. You can build with them, build upon them, lean upon them and even defend yourself with them. In the same way, many individuals are weak and useless. They may make a lot of noise and inflict much pain, but individuals, isolated from their brethren, accomplish little for the glory of God and the good of men's souls. But let us be bound together as one by the Spirit of God in Christ and we are strong, a mighty instrument for good in the hands of God.

Wherever men and women are united by grace into the fellowship of a gospel church, it is every member's responsibility to do what he or she can to keep the unity of the Spirit and the bond of peace. We must be careful not to grieve the Spirit of God by petty strife, slander, gossip, selfishness and childish peevishness (Eph. 4:30), and we must be careful to promote the unity and peace of God's saints.

Let our hearts be united in love for one another (Phil. 2:2). Let our opinions be united in the doctrine of the gospel (1 Cor. 1:10-11). Let our souls be united in the faith of Christ (Phil. 1:27). Let our spirits be united in the worship of our great God (Rom. 15:6). If in these things we are united, we will be at peace with one another. Therefore, 'Let nothing be done through strife or vainglory' (Phil. 2:3). There is no place in the body of Christ for proud, contentious, self-willed people. Promoters of strife and division are not welcome. Anyone who opposes the doctrine of the Word of God is not welcome. Those who preach free will or salvation by works and legalists are not welcome in the church of Christ. Those who seek religious entertainment, social activities and personal recognition will find nothing for them in the church of God. We are to seek nothing but the will of God, the Word of God and the worship of God. We must ever strive for peace if we desire that the God of peace be present with us in our assemblies of public worship (2 Cor. 13:11).

3. Members of Christ's church are to be sympathetic and kind to one another (Rom. 12:15)

Who does not need a little sympathy and kindness? Give it and you will receive it, pressed down, shaken together and running over. May the Lord graciously and constantly teach us to be kind and sympathetic towards our brethren in all the conditions and circumstances of their lives. Instead of seeking the sympathy and kindness of others, let us give sympathy and kindness to others. We are to help the needy, forgive the offending, comfort the troubled, support the weak, raise the fallen, sympathize with those in pain and enter into the joys of the blessed. In so doing we fulfil the law of Christ (Gal. 6:2, 9, 10).

4. If we are truly sympathetic and kind to one another, we will minister to one another's needs (Matt. 25:40)

God's children in this world have needs, and it is the responsibility of every believer to do what he or she can to relieve their needs.

The material, physical needs of God's family are the personal responsibility of each one of us (Rom. 12:13; Gal: 6:10; 1 John 3:17). We may not be able to provide luxuries, but we can provide the necessities of a brother. We may not be able to buy him a house, but we can buy him a few groceries. We may not be able to purchase a wardrobe for him, but we can buy him a coat. We may not be able to buy him a car, but we can buy him some gasoline. We are not responsible to do what God has not given us the ability to do, but we are all responsible to do what we can.

The emotional, spiritual needs of God's saints are also the responsibility of every believer (Gal. 6:2). We are to use the grace, experience, knowledge and faith God has given us to comfort, strengthen and edify his people.

Perhaps someone is asking, 'How can I minister to anyone?' You can tell others what you know, what God has done for you by his grace and what you have experienced of his goodness, and you can listen to them with a patient, caring, understanding heart.

5. The members of God's church are to watch over one another in love (Heb. 12:15)

We are not to spy on one another. We are not to be lords over the lives and consciences of God's people, but we are to watch over and watch out for one another. We are to watch for opportunities to help and encourage one another in the way of faith, supporting the weak, inspiring the faint, restoring the fallen. Do not look for opportunities to criticize, but for opportunities to care. Do not look for opportunities to slander, but for opportunities to serve. Do not look for opportunities to hurt, but for opportunities to help.

6. We are to forbear with and forgive one another for Christ's sake (Eph. 4:32; Col. 3:12-13)

Religious people lean hard upon one another. God's people are forbearing with one another, considering the patience, longsuffering and forbearance of God towards us. Let the strong support the weak. Let the offended forgive the offender. Let the faithful be patient with the unfaithful. Let the older help the younger. Let the mature nurture the infants.

Our patience is to be without limitation. Our forbearance is to be without qualification. Our forgiveness is to be without condition. Matthew 18:21-22 and Matthew 6:14-15 show us how we are to live with our brethren.

7. Members of the church are to pray for one another (Eph. 6.18)

People who love each other pray for each other, and it is very difficult to be hard, unkind, critical and unforgiving towards someone

for whom you are praying. We are to pray for our brothers and sisters
in Christ — that they may grow in the grace and knowledge of
Christ, that they may be kept from the evil one and preserved by
grace and that they may know the manifold blessings of God in
Christ continually.

We are to 'pray for the peace of Jerusalem' (Ps. 122:6-9), the
whole church of God. But each of us is to pray especially for that
little hill of Zion where we dwell, that local church of which we are
members, that peace may be within her walls and prosperity in the
house of God. Let us ever seek the good of God's people.

**8. Believers are responsible to separate themselves from the
world and unto the church of God** (2 Cor. 6:17-18).

The word 'church' means 'called out'. We have been called out of
and away from the world. We are not to be unequally yoked together
with unbelievers. Our own happiness, as well as the glory of God
and the cause of Christ, requires this separation. Voluntary en-
tanglement with the men and women of this world who do not know
and worship our God is always a great hindrance and detriment to
a believer. I do not mean that we should avoid contact with the
world. Isolationism is the height of hypocrisy and self-righteousness. But I do mean that we must avoid putting ourselves into the
same yoke with unbelievers. Let me specify.

*In all social affairs believers must form their alliances and associ-
ations with the children of God.* The ox and the ass cannot plough
well together. Whatever excuses we may make, the fact still remains
that 'Evil communications corrupt good manners . . .' Bad company
corrupts good principles. Good principles never improve bad company. If you would live peaceably in this world for the glory of God,
make your circle of friends the family of God, choose your husband
or wife from among God's saints and form your partnerships with
the servants of God.

*In all doctrinal and spiritual matters separation from the world is
essential.* We are to have no fellowship or association with anyone
who opposes the gospel of God's free and sovereign grace in Christ
(Rom. 16:17; 1 Tim. 6:3-5; Titus 3:10; 2 John 10-11). If we would

have God for our Father, we must come out of and renounce the religion of this world. There is no room in the house of God for free-will teaching, legalism or works religion of any kind! We must persistently reject the evil influence of the world's religion, and the best way to do that is to avoid association with those men and women who oppose our God and the gospel of his sovereign grace. We must have no more to do with them than Elijah would with the prophets of Baal.

9. It is the privilege and responsibility of every member of the church faithfully to attend the assembling of God's saints for public worship (Heb. 10:25)

As we saw in chapter 1, the first step towards total apostasy is the neglect of public worship. Hebrews 10:25-31 shows what a danger-ous thing it is to our souls to neglect the assembly of God's saints.

Who can tell what great blessing we might miss, when we neglect the assembly? Thomas could tell us! What evil might be avoided, what benefit might be given to those who do not neglect the ordinance of God?

10. In the church of God there must be no respect of persons (Rom. 12:10, 16)

Worldly honour, rank, wealth and power, race, social standing and education all count for nothing in the house of God. In God's house, all are equal. All are sinners saved by grace — nothing more! 'Christ is all and in all.' If there is strife in the church, let it not be to gain personal honour, but to give honour to others, each striving to honour and exalt the other and all striving to honour and exalt Christ. Let us always exalt the brother of low degree, honour the weak and magnify the poor. We must never give preference to any man or woman because of natural, social or financial superiority!

11. Every member must strive together with the rest and earnestly contend for the faith of the gospel (Jude 3)

Wherever we are, and whatever our particular gifts and abilities, we must each do what we can to proclaim and defend the gospel of

God's free and sovereign grace in Christ. We must make known to
the generation in which we live the glorious message of God's
sovereign mercy (Rom. 9:16), Christ's substitutionary atonement (2
Cor. 5:21) and salvation by grace alone (Eph. 2:8). Not all can
preach. But all can tell what they know, distribute tracts, give a tape
and bring people to hear the gospel preached. If we do what we can
for Christ, he will honour it.

**12. Members of the church are all responsible to be examples to
one another** (1 Tim. 4:12)

'Holiness,' writes John Gill, 'becomes the house of God, and the
members in it; their light should shine both in the church and in the
world, that others, beholding their good works, may imitate them,
and glorify God.'

Others in God's family, for whatever reason, are watching us,
following our example and imitating us. We must each be sure that
we set a good example, by being sound in faith, steadfast in doctrine,
faithful in behaviour, gracious in speech and loving in attitude.

In this chapter we have seen twelve practical admonitions which
the Scripture gives us to help us serve Christ, his gospel and his
church in this world. Let us make sure that we obey them for the
glory of God, the good of our brethren, the furtherance of the gospel
and the well-being of our own souls. Let us not give our adversaries
any occasion to blaspheme our God, speak reproachfully of our
Saviour, scandalize the gospel, or hold the church of God in
contempt (1 Tim. 3:15).

> Your people, Master, I would serve —
> Choose the best place for me;
> Give me the gifts most needed now,
> That I might useful be.
>
> My all I consecrate to you,
> My God, my sovereign Lord,
> Oh let me serve your cause on earth
> To spread your gracious Word.

Your church on earth I take to be
My family in this world;
A faithful member make of me,
To honour you, my God.

When I have served my usefulness
In your kingdom below,
I would to your triumphant church
In heaven's glory go.

There I shall serve you as I would,
With that great ransomed throng,
To whom I hope, by grace divine,
I rightfully belong.

13.
The Lord's Supper

'For I have received of the Lord that which also I delivered unto you, That the Lord Jesus the same night in which he was betrayed took bread: and when he had given thanks, he brake it, and said, Take, eat: this is my body, which is broken for you: this do in remembrance of me. After the same manner also he took the cup, when he had supped, saying, This cup is the new testament in my blood: this do ye, as oft as ye drink it, in remembrance of me. For as often as ye eat this bread, and drink this cup, ye do show the Lord's death till he come. Wherefore whosoever shall eat this bread, and drink this cup of the Lord, unworthily, shall be guilty of the body and blood of the Lord. But let a man examine himself, and so let him eat of that bread, and drink of that cup. For he that eateth and drinketh unworthily, eateth and drinketh damnation to himself, not discerning the Lord's body' (1 Cor. 11:23-39).

Perhaps the most blessed and most solemn ordinance of the gospel is the Lord's Supper. On the night before his crucifixion our Saviour gathered his disciples together in an upper room to eat the feast of the Passover. He was about to die as the true Passover Lamb for the atonement of our sins. The Jews ate the Passover supper in anticipation of redemption, as it was portrayed in the deliverance of Israel from the bondage of Egypt. And, on the eve of his crucifixion, our Saviour consecrated the supper to us as a memorial celebration of redemption by him. From that day to this, God's church has regularly met together to observe the Lord's Supper in happy, loving memory of our Redeemer, the Lord Jesus Christ, and the redemption he accomplished for us by his sacrificial, sin-atoning death at Jerusalem as our substitute. Every time we eat the bread and drink the wine we are declaring, to ourselves and to the world, that 'Christ our Passover is sacrificed for us' (1 Cor. 5:7).

Precious as this ordinance is, there is great need that God's elect have a clear understanding of its meaning and how it is to be observed. In this chapter I want to set out some plain and practical, biblical instruction about this blessed ordinance. In 1 Corinthians 11:23-29 the apostle Paul teaches us the meaning of this ordinance and tells us how and by whom it is to be observed.

There are three common errors about the Lord's Supper that must be set aside.

1. *The bread and wine of the Lord's Table do not become, either literally or spiritually, the body and blood of Christ.* Those elements represent our Saviour's body and blood, but they only represent our Lord. They picture Christ, but they do not become Christ!

2. *The Lord's Supper is not a sacrament, a means by which grace is conveyed to sinners.* It has absolutely no saving efficacy. It is not a means by which people obtain grace and favour with God. Those who are not born of God, those who have no faith in the Lord Jesus Christ, are not to eat the bread and drink the wine of the Lord's Table. Like baptism, this ordinance is for believers only.

3. *The Lord's Supper is not strictly a local church ordinance.* It is administered by the local church in the name of Christ, but it is not an ordinance limited to the members of the church administering it, and the local church has no right to place limitations, qualifications, or restrictions upon those who receive the ordinance which are not spelt out in the New Testament. It is not the church's supper; it is the Lord's Supper, and, as such, it is open to all the Lord's children. In Acts 20:1-7 disciples from many different cities, meeting together in one place on the Lord's Day, observed the Lord's Supper together, though they were not members of the same local church.

What is the Lord's Supper?

It is a symbolic representation of the believer's redemption by the death of the Lord Jesus Christ. As Israel remembered the Passover and their deliverance out of Egypt by keeping the feast, so our Lord commands us to keep this memorial feast as a regular, visible reminder of our redemption by him. Therefore he took the bread and wine at hand and established this feast as a perpetual ordinance in his church and kingdom. Like baptism, this is an ordinance both practised and commanded by our Master. It was maintained after his death by the apostles and early churches, and it is to be observed by us until Christ comes again.

Let us try to picture in our minds that upper room in Jerusalem. There sits the Lord Jesus with his disciples. He has told them all that he must suffer for our sake, how that he must die as our substitute and then rise from the dead and ascend back into heaven. What a solemn assembly that must have been! What a privilege to have been there! These favoured disciples hung upon every word the Saviour spoke and took notice of every gesture. The King of glory was talking and eating with his little band of loyal subjects for the last time before his death, and they all knew it. As he spoke to them, he took a loaf of bread and declared it to be an emblem of his body. He blessed it, gave thanks for it and asked God's blessing upon it. Then he broke the loaf. By breaking that loaf of bread, the Lord Jesus showed how that his body must be bruised, torn and crushed beneath the wrath of God. Then he gave the bread to his disciples, saying, 'Take, eat, this is my body.' Each disciple took the bread with his own hand and ate it, just as they had each taken Christ by the hand of faith and fed upon him.

Then he took the wine, the emblem of his blood. He blessed it, drank it and passed the cup to each of his disciples, saying, 'This cup is the New Testament [New Covenant (Jer. 31:31-34)] in my blood: this do ye, as oft as ye drink it, in remembrance of me.' Thus our Redeemer showed his willingness and readiness to pour out his life's blood unto death for the remission of our sins.

To this day the church of God observes this same supper, using the same elements, for the same purpose, to show forth the Lord's death until he comes again.

Who should observe the Lord's Supper?

All true believers. It is the Lord's Table, and the Lord's Table is open to all the Lord's children (Acts 20:1-2). The practice of restricting the Lord's Supper to the members of a single local church, or denomination, or even to those who meet certain requirements legislated by a church, is altogether without foundation in the Word of God. Each believer is to examine himself, and having examined himself, he is to eat the bread and drink the wine. It is not the prerogative of the pastor, elders, deacons, or the church to examine those who receive the Lord's Supper. Not only is the Lord's Table open to all the Lord's children, but all his children are commanded by him to eat the bread and drink the wine (Matt. 26: 26-27). This ordinance is no more optional than the ordinance of baptism.

Many of God's children have been taught to fear coming to the Lord's Table. Many people in conservative, sovereign grace churches seem to think that they show great reverence for the ordinance by not participating in it! This attitude is not really reverence at all, but irreverence, for it is disobedience to the command of our Lord Jesus Christ.

Many refuse to receive the Lord's Supper because they feel unworthy. But our worthiness is not in ourselves, but in Christ. We come to the table not with personal perfection, but with personal faith. By eating the bread and drinking the wine, we show our confidence in the finished work of Christ to make us accepted in God's sight. In all things, our only worthiness to approach and draw near to the holy God is Christ (Heb. 10:19-22; Eph. 1:6; 1 Peter 2:5). Our worthiness to pray, sing praises to God, give, preach, eat the Lord's Supper, or do anything else towards God is the righteousness of Christ imputed to us and the blood of Christ applied to us. Our only acceptance with God is Christ (Col. 2:9-10). Those who are united to Christ are worthy to receive the bread and wine, because they discern the Lord's body. They know their need of a substitute and understand how that Christ accomplished redemption by his incarnation and obedience unto death.

Clearly, there are some people who should not be partakers of this ordinance. Paul gives strong warning to those who might be so brazen as to come presumptuously to the Lord's Table to eat and drink unworthily (1 Cor. 11:27-29). The question is: who is un-worthy? Unbelievers are unworthy to eat the Lord's Supper, and professed believers whose lives are a scandalous reproach to Christ and the gospel of his grace are unworthy to eat the supper. Their unworthiness lies in the fact that they do not discern the Lord's body, that is to say, they do not know the meaning and value of Christ's incarnation, his righteous obedience to God as our representative and his sacrificial death as the sinner's substitute, because they have no faith in him.

However, every true believer may and should come to the Lord's Table. I do not pretend to understand fully Paul's statements about unworthy recipients of the supper in 1 Corinthians 11. But I do know this: the Lord's Table is open to all the Lord's children. The practice of excluding members of other churches from the table has neither precept nor precedent in the New Testament. All God's children in this world are welcome to sit with his saints in any place where they gather to observe the Lord's Supper.

I have already said that the Lord's Supper is not a sacrament, but to the believer it is a blessed means of grace. There is never a time when the child of God is made more fully aware of his own sinfulness and his utter dependence upon Christ and his redemptive work than he is when he eats the Lord's Supper in faith. Every time we eat the bread and drink the wine we are confronted with our sin, comforted with a sense of blood-bought pardon and cheered with the hope of Christ's glorious second advent.

Paul also makes it perfectly clear that the person receiving the Lord's Supper is responsible to examine himself (1 Cor. 11:28). Each person must examine him or herself. Are you a believer? Do you discern the Lord's body? Do you see the value of Christ's incarnation, life of obedience and sin-atoning death? Do you rest your soul upon Christ by faith? If you do, this blessed gospel ordinance is for you, but if you refuse to trust the Son of God, you must not presume to take the bread and wine of the Lord's Supper.

What are the elements to be used in the Lord's Supper?

The Lord's Supper is to be observed by eating unleavened bread and drinking wine. Many churches and preachers substitute crackers or ordinary bread for unleavened bread and grape juice or other soft drinks for wine when serving the Lord's Supper. But such substitutions reveal a failure to understand the true meaning of this holy ordinance. Why must we use unleavened bread and wine? I will give you three reasons.

Firstly, when Melchizedek, who was a type of Christ, met Abraham, he brought forth bread and wine as the symbols of God's blessing through a sacrifice (Gen. 14:18-20).

Secondly, these were the elements used by our Lord and the early churches. At the Passover feast, which the Lord was observing when he instituted this ordinance, unleavened bread and wine were served.

Many of those who object to using wine in the supper do so because they have the false notion that the Bible forbids the use of alcoholic beverages. It does not. Our Lord did not turn water into grape juice at Cana. He turned it into wine (John 2:9). Were it wrong for men and women to drink wine, our Saviour would not have made it. And the Corinthians certainly did not get drunk by drinking too much grape juice at the Lord's Table!

Thirdly, we should use unleavened bread and wine because of the symbolic nature of the ordinance.

What is signified by the bread and wine?

The unleavened bread symbolizes the perfect, sinless humanity of our Saviour. It represents Christ's holy body. In order for the Son of God to be our Saviour, he had to assume our nature and live in perfect obedience to the law of God as a man, as our representative. Our Lord Jesus had no original sin. He had no actual sin. And he brought in a perfect, everlasting righteousness for us by his obedience to God in the body of his flesh. That bread which is without leaven represents Christ's body, which is without sin. The breaking of the bread represents the crushing of our Lord's body in death, under the wrath of God, to accomplish our redemption.

The pure, fermented wine fitly represents the precious, sin-atoning blood of Christ, by which our sins have been washed away and the covenant of grace has been ratified. The blood of our redemption was not 'divine' blood, but nor was it ordinary human blood. It was the blood of the spotless Lamb of God. It was the blood of the incarnate God. It was the blood of a man who is God! The wine, having all impurity removed by the process of fermentation, symbolizes the purity of Christ's blood. Its ruby colour represents the richness of the covenant of grace, and its taste reminds us of the sweetness of our Savour's love.

The bread and wine separated signify the death of our Lord Jesus. When the blood is separated from the body death is certain. As the wine comes from grapes which have been crushed in the winepress, the precious blood of Christ gushed out of his body, when he was crushed beneath the wheel of divine justice in the winepress of God's holy wrath as our substitute. The two, bread and wine, the body and the blood, separated, tell us that justice is satisfied, judgement is past, redemption is accomplished and our sins are gone. The bread and the wine declare, 'There is therefore now no condemnation to them that are in Christ Jesus' (Rom. 8:1).

3. Why do we observe this ordinance?

If we are to observe the Lord's Supper properly, we must know why we do it. If it is nothing but a religious duty, a ritual, or a traditional ceremony to us, it is at best meaningless. If we place any kind of mystical, superstitious power upon the observance of the ordinance, make it a means of obtaining salvation or a method of appeasing God, the observance of the Lord's Supper becomes a blasphemous act of idolatry.

    We must, in all things, follow the example and command of our Lord. But obedience to Christ requires that we know why we do what we do in his worship and service. Here are four reasons why we keep the feast of the Lord's Supper.

1. *Our Lord commands us to observe it* (Matt. 26:26-28; Mark 14:22-24; Luke 22:19-20; 1 Cor. 11:24-25). Our Saviour said, 'This do ye.' It is as much the command of Christ for believers to eat the bread and drink the wine of the Lord's Supper as it is for us to be baptized in his name. The ordinances of Christ are not optional. He commands every believer to observe the Lord's Supper.

2. *The Lord's Supper is to be observed in remembrance of Christ.* He says, 'This do in remembrance of me.' When a beloved companion has been gone for a long time, our hearts rejoice in the

remembrance of his or her words, actions, ways and gestures. Memory of these things heightens our anticipation of the loved one's return. And we observe this ordinance of the gospel in remembrance of our Saviour, anticipating his return. As we eat the bread and drink the wine, our hearts swell with the hope that the Lord Jesus will soon appear! When we observe this ordinance, let us remember the Saviour with love and faith.

We remember *his glorious person*. He is very God of very God, and he is also a real man, a man of flesh and blood, just like us, with one great exception — he is without sin! We remember his great condescension. 'For ye know the grace of our Lord Jesus Christ, that, though he was rich, yet for your sakes he became poor, that ye through his poverty might be rich' (2 Cor. 8:9). We remember his humble obedience, the temptations he endured, his agony in Gethsemane and his death upon the cursed tree. How blessed it is to go again and again to the place called Calvary and remember our Lord! His words of grace, his redeeming love, his precious blood and the glorious success of his work upon the cross are things that charm our hearts. We remember too the triumphant resurrection, glorious ascension, heavenly intercession and sovereign dominion of Christ, the God-man, our Mediator.

Perhaps the best way to remember Christ's person is to remember *his gracious works*. His electing love (John 15:16), his covenant engagements (Heb. 10:5-10), his merciful deliverances (2 Cor. 1:10) and his advocacy for us (1 John 2:1-2) are things that fill our hearts with comfort, assurance and praise.

Nor must we fail to remember *his great promises*. He has promised us his constant presence (Matt. 28:20), his omniscient direction (Prov. 3:5-6), his omnipotent protection (John 10:27-30), his bountiful provision (Matt. 6:33-34), his perfect peace (John 14:27), his sure return (John 14:1-4) and the perfect completion of our salvation in resurrection glory (John 10:16; Eph. 5:25-27). What could be more precious, beneficial and reviving to our souls than the remembrance of our dear Saviour? And to make certain that we remember him, he gave us this blessed ordinance and said, 'This do in remembrance of me!'

3. *We are to observe the ordinance of the Lord's Supper as a testimony to those who do not know our Saviour.* This is not an ordinance to be observed in secret. It is a public ordinance. 'For as

often as ye eat this bread, and drink this cup, ye do show the Lord's death till he come' (1 Cor. 11:26). The Lord's Supper is a gospel sermon in a picture. We show all who see us observing it how that Christ became a man and suffered the wrath of God unto death for the redemption of sinners. As we take the bread and wine, we show the necessity of personal faith in the Son of God (John 6:54). We also declare to all men that the Saviour whose memory we cherish will soon come again.

4. *Our observance of the Lord's Supper is a celebration of redemption.* It is a solemn service, but it is a joyful celebration! Every time we eat the bread and drink the wine, we are celebrating the accomplishment of redemption by Christ. By his blood, satisfying divine justice, Christ has redeemed us from the curse of the law, the penalty of sin (Gal. 3:13). By the effectual power of his Spirit he has saved us from the power of sin in regenerating grace (Eph. 2:1-5). And soon our dear Saviour will come again to save us from the presence and all the consequences of sin, by the power of his resurrection (Jude 24-25).

When should we observe the Lord's Supper?

The Scriptures do not prescribe any fixed time when the ordinance must be observed. Therefore we must not presume to do so. But some things appear to be obvious.

It seems reasonable to me that since it is the Lord's Supper, not the Lord's Breakfast, it should be observed in the evening, as it was originally (Mark 14:17). Because our Lord was raised from the dead on Sunday, and because his apostles and the early churches observed the supper on Sunday, we should do so too. And, since the early churches in the book of Acts observed the Lord's Supper every Lord's Day, we should do the same.

I have been convinced of these things for many years. In the church I pastor, this is the way we keep the Lord's Supper, and I see no reason to make any change. However, these things are not required, nor commanded, anywhere in the New Testament. Therefore it would be wrong for me, or anyone else, to insist that all local churches observe the Lord's Supper every Sunday evening. No such suggestion is implied!

But some things are commanded and must not be altered.

The Lord's Table is to be set before the Lord's people often (1 Cor. 11:25). Many churches observe this ordinance only once or twice a year. I know of one congregation in which God's saints were deprived of the Lord's Supper for twelve years! This is an intolerably evil neglect of Christ's command. We are to observe his ordinance often!

We are to observe the Lord's Supper collectively, as a body of believers, gathered in the church (1 Cor. 11:33; Acts 20:7). This ordinance is not to be observed by individuals. I cannot find any precedent for such conduct in the Scriptures. We observe the ordinance collectively, as the church of God, because one aspect of the supper is the unity of God's saints as one body in Christ (1 Cor. 10:16-17). That can be expressed by two or three believers together, but it cannot be expressed by one person alone.

The church of God is to observe the Lord's Supper often, until Christ comes again (1 Cor. 11:26). Every time God's saints meet around the table, we are reminded of the fact that Christ is absent from us. He is not physically with us, but we are filled with joy in anticipation of the thought that soon he will come again. Every time I place the bread in my mouth and put the wine to my lips, I try to think to myself, 'Perhaps before I swallow this bread and wine, the Lord Jesus will appear in glory!' With that thought I conclude every Lord's Day and begin every week.

It is my prayer that these words of instruction will be blessed of God to all who read them, so that they may be able to eat the bread and drink the wine of this holy ordinance with a fuller appreciation and greater joy than they have known before. When we come to the Lord's Table with God's saints, let us set our hearts upon the remembrance of our blessed Redeemer. Let our hearts go out to the Lord Jesus in expressions of deep gratitude, fervent love, firm faith and full devotion. And as we sit with God's people in holy communion, let us each resolve to do what we can to keep the unity of the Spirit in the bond of peace.

14.
Coming together in church

'When ye come together in the church...' (1 Cor. 11:18)

In 1 Corinthians 11 the apostle Paul gives the believers at Corinth instructions about church order, particularly about the observance of the Lord's Supper. He tells us that certain things are essential in the worship of God. If we would worship God in the celebration of the Lord's Supper, we must observe the ordinance as God requires. Otherwise, the ordinance is a meaningless ritual.

What the apostle teaches regarding the Lord's Supper is true of every aspect of public worship. Whenever and wherever God's saints assemble in the name of Christ, 'when ye come together in the church' to worship God, some things are essential. If we would truly worship the Lord our God when we come together as a body of believers, we must worship him 'after the due order' (1 Chron. 15:13). Otherwise, our services of public worship are empty, meaningless, bodily exercises of no profit (1 Tim. 4:8).

I am afraid that the vast majority of religious people perform their religious exercises in an utterly careless form of worship. Like the Samaritans, most people worship they know not what. Their worship is without God, without Christ, without the Spirit, without knowledge, without faith and without heart. Such worship is not only of no benefit to the soul, it is positively harmful. The church of this modern 'enlightened' age needs some plain, practical, biblical instruction about public worship.

As I have already said, some things are essential to public worship. Where these things are present, there is worship. Where these essential things are absent, worship is defective and incomplete, to say the least.

1. True worship is an act of faith

Public worship, as well as private, is a work of faith. No one can worship God apart from personal faith in the Lord Jesus Christ. This is the first matter of importance. If we would worship God, we must trust Christ. We come to God only by faith in Christ (Heb. 7:25). The Lord Jesus himself declares, 'I am the way, the truth, and the life; no man cometh unto the Father, but by me' (John 14:6).

Without question, the great God with whom we have to do is infinitely kind, gracious and tender. 'God is love.' But he is also infinitely just, pure and holy. He is righteous and true. God has an infinite hatred of sin. He cannot endure that which is evil. He cast one third of the angels out of heaven because of sin. He once drowned the world in a flood because of his wrath against sin. He burned Sodom and Gomorrah in furious anger because of sin. And any who carelessly presume to approach him without the atonement and Mediator whom he has appointed, any who attempt to approach him without faith in Christ, will find that our 'God is a consuming fire' (Heb. 12:29). We must be washed in the blood of Christ and robed in his righteousness by faith, or we cannot worship God.

2. True worship must be knowledgeable worship

I do not mean that worshippers must be educated, or that they must be theologians, but I do mean that in order to worship God a person must know what he is doing.

The Athenians superstitiously worshipped an 'unknown God' (Acts 17:23), and our Lord said of the Samaritans, 'Ye worship ye know not what' (John 4:22); but true believers know the God they worship and they know why they worship him. We worship the great and glorious, sovereign and holy God in the trinity of his sacred persons (1 John 5:7); and we worship him because he is a God worthy of worship (Ps. 115:1-3). We worship God the Father as our

heavenly Father because of his eternal grace. We worship God the
Son as our blessed Saviour because of his redemptive work. We
worship God the Spirit as our divine Comforter because of his
comforting mercy.

If we would worship God, we must worship him in the
knowledge of the truth (John 4:24). If we would worship God we
must know something of ourselves, our depravity, guilt, sin and
inability (Matt. 15:19; Heb. 11:6), something about God's holy,
righteous, sovereign character (Isa. 45:20-25), something about the
person and work of Christ as our surety, substitute, mediator and
King (2 Cor. 5:21; Heb. 10:5-14), and something of the grace and
power of God the Holy Spirit (John 6:63; Eph. 1:13-14).

3. True worship is an act of the heart

The essence of true worship, both private and public, is heart
worship. It is not enough simply to 'attend church', going through
the mental and physical exercises of outward worship. Our hearts
must be employed in the worship of God (Isa. 29:13; Matt. 15:8;
Ezek. 33:31). The heart is the principal thing. If we do not worship
God in our hearts, all our outward deeds, services and sacrifices are
worthless. They are worse than worthless. Outward service without
inward worship is hypocrisy and an abomination to God! 'Man
looketh on the outward appearance, but the Lord looketh on the
heart' (1 Sam. 16:7). The broken and contrite heart is the sacrifice
which God will not despise (Ps. 51:17). He says, 'Give me thine
heart' (Prov. 23:26).

God looks beyond the outward acts of religious devotion to the
heart. We dare not neglect the outward ordinances, but the outward
ordinance without the heart is nothing.

4. True worship requires reverence

Worship implies adoration, reverence and solemnity. 'God is
greatly to be feared in the assembly of the saints, and to be had in
reverence of all them that are about him' (Ps. 89:7). If we would
worship God acceptably, we must worship him with 'reverence and
godly fear' (Heb. 12:28). There is no place in the house of God for

flippancy, levity, or the mere show of emotionalism. Anything that calls attention to ourselves is out of place in the house of God, whether it be outbursts of emotionalism or showy forms of dress. Anything that distracts from the ministry of the Word and the worship of God is not to be tolerated in the assembly of God's saints. God detests profane carelessness and indifference in his presence. He will not tolerate it. J. C. Ryle said, 'People who call themselves Christians, and go to churches and chapels to stare about, whisper, fidget, yawn, or sleep, but not to pray, praise, and listen, are not a whit better than the wicked Jews,' who bought and sold in the temple. If it is worthwhile to come to the house of God, it is worthwhile to do so with careful reverence. 'Let us have grace, whereby we may serve God acceptably with reverence and godly fear' (Heb. 12:28). God requires reverence of those who come into his house (Eccles. 5:1).

When we come together with God's saints for public worship, we should remember that we are coming into the house of God to hear from and worship God Almighty in all the splendour, beauty and glory of his holy being. We must see that we give him the reverence of our hearts.

We must come prepared to worship. We should prepare our hearts, our bodies and our minds to worship God. This may mean cutting out some weekend recreation, or curtailing our hours of work, in order to get enough rest so that we do not come to the house of God tired and sleepy. If people stay up late on Saturday night, sleep late on Sunday morning and rush into the house of God without thought or preparation of heart, they are not likely to worship God. More often than not, their minds will wander in a thousand directions until, weary from lack of rest, they go to sleep. God deserves better!

We must come promptly to the place of worship. Men and women have a thousand excuses for being late for worship services, but these same people get to work every day on time, get their children dressed, fed and off to school on time and get to an appointment at the doctor's on time. Why do people persistently come to the house of God late? Because they do not consider the worship of God to be a matter of great importance. If our souls, the gospel of Christ, the worship of Christ and the glory of Christ are important to us, we will arrange to come to the house of God with promptness.

Would you be late for an appointment with the President of the United States, the Queen of England, or any dignitary? Tardiness for such an appointment would be embarrassing to you and intolerable before your royal host. Dare you treat the King of heaven with less regard?

We must come praying for grace to worship. We should seek grace from the Lord to worship in the Spirit. We are to pray for God to speak to our hearts through his Word, in the prayers that are offered and by the songs that are sung. We are to pray for those who lead the congregation in worship, that they may be led of the Spirit, and for the man who preaches the gospel, that he may preach in power. We should pray for ourselves and our brethren, that we may see, hear, worship and obey the Lord Jesus Christ.

We must come to the house of God for prayer and praise. We must be prepared to worship when we come. We are to put the cares of the world, as much as possible, out of our minds, and sit before the throne of God with humility, wonder, attention and reverence. No disturbances or distractions of any kind are to be tolerated. It is unthinkable that men and women who hold God in reverence would run in and out, talk, allow their children to play, or disrupt the worship of God with crying babies, while the Word of God is being read, the praise of God is being sung, the message of God is being delivered or the throne of God is being supplicated!

5. Our worship of God must be according to the Scriptures

God will not accept any worship, no matter how costly, sincere, or fervent, that is not according to the Scriptures. Most of that which men call worship today is an abomination to God. Our Lord said, 'In vain they do worship me, teaching for doctrines the commandments of men' (Matt. 15:9). That which is not according to the Scriptures Paul calls 'a show of wisdom in will worship... to the satisfying of the flesh' (Col. 2:23).

I recognize that the New Testament does not give detailed instruction regarding the proper order of our worship services. The typical, ceremonial ordinances of worship in the Old Testament were strictly regulated in every detail by the law of God, because every aspect of worship in the Old Testament pointed to and foreshadowed the redemptive work of Christ, but the New Testament allows much more freedom.

We have no right to invent our own ordinances of worship, no right to add to what God requires, no right to neglect what God requires and no right to alter what God requires. However, we are free to choose the place, time and order of our services for public worship, according to our circumstances, needs and preferences. The Word of God makes no requirements in these matters.

Yet anyone who reads the New Testament attentively cannot fail to see that whenever and wherever God's saints met together in the name of Christ for worship, they always practised certain things. Here are four things which should be done without fail, and with great care, every time the church meets for public worship.

1. A prominent place must be given to the public reading of Holy Scripture

No part of the worship service is more important than the reading of the Word of God. When the Scriptures are read, we receive direct, verbally inspired instruction from God himself.

In twenty years of pastoral work I have never conducted a public worship service without giving a special place to the reading of God's Word, and I never intend to do so. I consider it to be as important as prayer, praise and preaching.

In the synagogue worship of the Jews a prominent place was given to the reading of Holy Scripture every sabbath day (Luke 4:16; Acts 13:15). The apostle Paul told the young pastor, Timothy, to give attendance to reading the Scriptures, exhorting the saints and teaching the doctrine of the gospel (1 Tim. 4:13). That is the way preachers are supposed to conduct the services of public worship. The epistles of the New Testament were written to be read in the churches, and our Lord's letters to the churches of Asia (Rev. 2-3) were to be read to the churches.

I cannot overstress the importance of this practice. In every local church there are some who either cannot or do not read the Word of God for themselves, and some who read so poorly that they do not read correctly. Reason and common sense should teach us the usefulness of publicly reading the Scriptures to them. If men and women are to worship God, they must know what God says in his Word. God's Word alone, not the preacher's comments about it, is inspired and authoritative (2 Tim. 3:16-17). Therefore prominence should be given to the reading of Holy Scripture in every assembly of the church. Hezekiah Harvey says, 'The omission of this would imply that the words of man are of higher moment than the words of God. The Scriptures should have a large and reverent use in the pulpit, as the fountain of all instruction and the sole standard of faith and practice.'

Primarily, it is the pastor's responsibility to read the Scriptures to the congregation. When he does, he may choose a passage relating to his message for the hour and give a brief exposition as he reads. But such expositions should always be carefully prepared, so that he does no violence to the text. Spontaneous, unprepared comments are seldom either accurate or helpful and display a terrible lack of reverence for the Word of God.

The pastor may ask one of the men of the church to read the Scriptures. If anyone is asked to do so, he must not take the work lightly, for he has the responsibility of reading God's Word to his people. The portion he chooses to read and the way he reads it will set the tone for the entire worship service. He must seek the direction of God's Spirit with care. I make the following recommendations to anyone entrusted with this task.

Select a devotional passage, a portion of Scripture that will lead the hearts of God's people to Christ. Select a brief passage. Generally, it is best to select just one passage. And always select a passage by which God has spoken to your own heart.

Familiarize yourself with the passage you plan to read. Read it carefully, prayerfully and studiously at home. Read it several times, noting the punctuation of the text. Be certain that you understand the portion of Scripture you read to the church. If you do not understand it, select another portion to read.

Read the passage carefully and distinctly. Remember you are not reading for yourself alone. You are reading to the congregation. Read loudly enough that everyone present can hear you distinctly! If you are not accustomed to reading in public, read the passage aloud at home. It is frustrating to try to follow a reading that cannot be heard.

Read the Word of God without comment. Leave it to the preacher to do the preaching. When the Scriptures are read it is so that God's people may hear God speak to their hearts by his Word.

2. The congregation should be united and led to the throne of grace in public prayer in every worship service (1 Tim. 2:1-4)

Paul gives this exhortation: 'That, first of all, supplications, prayers, intercessions, and giving of thanks, be made for all men.' We are to make 'supplications' to God for the grace we need. We make our 'prayers' to God for his blessings upon his people, his servants around the world, the missionary efforts of the church, other churches, etc. We make 'intercessions' to God for the needs of others: needy saints, sinful men, those who are in places of political authority and the man who must preach the gospel. And we offer the 'giving of thanks' to God for the grace we have experienced, the mercy we need and the promises he has made.

These are the things which should occupy our hearts when we are engaged in public prayer. I cannot stress enough the importance of public prayer. Any time a man is called upon to lead the congregation to the throne of grace in prayer, he is called upon to do that which is of the greatest importance and benefit to the church of God. It should never be taken lightly. The one praying is leading God's saints in the worship of God. Public prayer is the worship of the whole church through the voice of one man, chosen to represent and speak for the whole congregation. When anyone is called upon to lead the church in prayer, it is not only that he may speak to God for the church, but also that he may stimulate the thoughts and desires of God's people, so that their hearts may be quickened and led heavenwards to Christ.

When a man is called upon to lead the congregation in prayer, let him be aware of what he is doing. He is leading the assembly of God to the throne of grace to seek God's blessing upon the service. He is speaking to God, so let his words be few, thoughtfully chosen and earnest. He is calling upon God in prayer, so let him be sincere,

believing and conscious of the needs of the hour. He is leading the
congregation, so let him speak distinctly and loudly enough to be
heard by all. He cannot lead the church in prayer, if the church
cannot hear him. He should pray with thoughtful reverence and
sincerity, with fervent faith and submissively, willingly submitting
everything, every request and every desire to the will of God and the
glory of God (see Matt. 6:9-13).

3. United public praise is essential to public worship (Eph. 5:19; Col. 3:16)

The service of song is important. The congregation should be led in
singing 'psalms', inspired hymns of the Scriptures, 'hymns' of
praise to God, written to extol his person and works, and 'spiritual
songs' of devotion, expressing faith, hope and love, as well as the
desires of our hearts towards God.

Someone has said, 'Praise is the flower of devotion.' Praise is
the only part of public worship that will continue in eternity. In
heaven's glory reading, praying and preaching will not be needed,
but our songs of praise will continue for ever.

Special music, by gifted men and women, is important and
beneficial. Instrumental music is also useful, but we must never
dispense with, or minimize, the importance of congregational
singing. All the saints of God are to sing unto the Lord and unto one
another. The singing is not musical recreation, or an artistic recital.
We do not come to the house of God to entertain people. In the
singing of the church a body of believers, united in faith, lift their
hearts and voices together in the praise and worship of the triune
God.

Every song that is sung in the church should be *selected carefully*, making certain that the message of the song is consistent with
the gospel of God's free and sovereign grace in Christ. Regrettably,
many hymn books include a number of songs which exalt free will
and the works of the flesh, or where truth is sacrificed in the interests
of sentimentality. Therefore a song leader must be very selective.
No song should ever be sung which is not doctrinally accurate! The
words of our hymns are to be *sung thoughtfully*, so that, while we
sing, we enter into the message of the song. The songs are to be *sung*

by all the congregation. Every member of the assembly should join in public praise, singing as unto the Lord.

4. Every time God's saints gather for worship the public preaching of the gospel must be the paramount feature of the worship service

Preaching is the work of the church. Without the preaching of the gospel, everything else is empty, meaningless and pointless. Everything done in public worship, the reading of the Word, the prayers offered and the hymns of praise must all serve, lead to and complement the preaching of the gospel.

In many churches preaching is an insignificant part of the worship service. More time is spent making announcements, raising money and recognizing people than is spent in preaching. If the preacher dares to speak for more than twenty or thirty minutes, he is sure to be in trouble, and too often preachers let themselves be intimidated by the men who hold their purse strings! Yet gospel preaching is God's ordained means of ministering to the needs of his people (Eph. 4:11-14). God saves sinners by the foolishness of preaching, and God speaks to, instructs, feeds, guides, edifies and comforts his children by the preaching of the gospel. Show me a strong church, whose members are well instructed in gospel truth, and I will show you a strong pulpit ministry. Show me a weak church, whose members are spiritually ignorant, and I will show you a weak pulpit ministry. If we would worship God in our assemblies, we must hear from God; and if we would hear from God, we must hear him speak through the voice of his servant preaching the gospel.

In God's house, among God's people and with God's servants, gospel preaching should be the matter of greatest importance in public worship. If it is not the matter of greatest importance where you attend church, I suggest that you find another church to attend!

The constant, singular theme of the pulpit is Jesus Christ and him crucified (1 Cor. 1:23; 2:1-2; 2 Cor. 5:19-21). All true preaching has a real and direct relation to Christ crucified. Christ crucified is the source, the centre, the substance and the end of all true preaching.

No topic is fit for any pulpit which does not lead men and women to Christ.

The preacher's theme never changes. In all ages, in all societies, in all cultures, in all circumstances, Christ crucified is our message (1 Cor. 9:16). Our message never changes because the depravity of man never changes (Jer. 17:9), the character of God never changes (Mal. 3:6), God's remedy for sin never changes (Isa. 45:22), and the believer's portion never changes (Lam. 3:24).

Certainly, I do not mean to imply that the preacher should neglect any subject, doctrine or text of Holy Scripture, but I am saying that every subject, every doctrine and every text of the Bible is preached properly and truly only when it leaves men and women looking to, trusting and worshipping the Lord Jesus Christ (Luke 24:27, 44-47; 1 Peter 1:25). Many men preach the Bible verse by verse, chapter by chapter and book by book, who never preach the message of the Bible. The message of the Bible is Jesus Christ and him crucified!

It is a sad fact that many who read these pages will probably be asking as they read, 'What is it to preach Jesus Christ and him crucified?' The religion of our day has been reduced to such a level that few, in the pulpit or in the pew, know the answer to that question. When the apostles declared, 'We preach Christ crucified' (1 Cor. 1:23) their meaning was: 'We preach Christ as the sum and substance of Holy Scripture, the source, foundation and cause of all grace, the sovereign Ruler of all things and the singular object of all true faith.'

The great object and goal of gospel preaching is the glory of God in Christ. The whole purpose of public worship is to lead men and women in the worship of the Lord God our Saviour. And that is the object of preaching. We preach the gospel so that all men may know who God is and what he has done in the person and work of his dear Son Jesus Christ our Lord. It is by this means alone that God saves his elect, comforts his children, edifies his saints and builds his kingdom.

15.
Hearing the Word of God

'Every good gift and every perfect gift is from above, and cometh down from the Father of lights, with whom is no variableness, neither shadow of turning. Of his own will begat he us with the word of truth, that we should be a kind of firstfruits of his creatures. Wherefore, my beloved brethren, let every man be swift to hear, slow to speak, slow to wrath; for the wrath of man worketh not the righteousness of God. Wherefore lay apart all filthiness and super-fluity of naughtiness, and receive with meekness the engrafted word, which is able to save your souls. But be ye doers of the word, and not hearers only, deceiving your own selves. For if any be a hearer of the word, and not a doer, he is like unto a man beholding his natural face in a glass: for he beholdeth himself, and goeth his way, and straightway forgetteth what manner of man he was. But whoso looketh into the perfect law of liberty, and continueth therein, he being not a forgetful hearer, but a doer of the work, this man shall be blessed in his deed' (James 1:17-25).

The greatest blessing God can bestow upon any town, or community, in this world is to raise up a gospel church in its midst, with a
pastor who preaches the gospel of Christ in its doctrinal purity and
in the power of the Holy Spirit. How blessed are those people who
have the privilege of hearing the Word of God preached with
boldness, in simplicity, with sincerity! How blessed are those men
and women who have a faithful pastor, who preaches the gospel of
Christ, without considering either the fear or the favour of men!

How blessed of God is that town which has a congregation of God's saints in its midst, a church where the pure doctrine of the gospel is preached!

There are few places in this world where men and women can go to hear, and know that they will hear, the gospel of the grace of God in Jesus Christ. The absolute sovereignty of God, the total depravity of man, the unconditional election of grace, the effectual atonement of Christ, the irresistible call of the Spirit and the infallible preservation and perseverance of God's saints should be the staple diet of every pulpit. But few preachers dare mention these things, much less preach upon them.

I am afraid that very few people know the value of a faithful gospel ministry. Even those who are so highly favoured of God that they have the Word of the Lord in their midst rarely value it as they should. A good friend of mine said to me recently, 'God gave us a faithful pastor. But we didn't appreciate him until he was taken away from us.'

I say again, without hesitation, a faithful pastor, a man who preaches the gospel of God's free and sovereign grace in Christ, is the greatest blessing God can bestow upon men and women in this world. And the greatest curse God can bring upon a people this side of hell is for him to silence the voice of his servant and remove the light of the gospel from their midst (see Amos 8:11-12). If, in this day of religious darkness and almost universal apostasy, God has given you a place where you can go to hear the gospel preached, you are blessed of God! Such a privilege ought to be cherished and guarded. But great privileges bring great responsibilities. And hearing the Word of God is a responsibility not to be taken lightly.

This is the subject James discusses in chapter 1:17-25. 'Every good gift and every perfect gift is from above, and cometh down from the Father of lights, with whom is no variableness, neither shadow of turning.' And among these good gifts, the best and most highly valued is the preaching of the gospel. This is God's ordained means of saving sinners. James says, 'Of his own will begat he us with the word of truth, that we should be a kind of firstfruits of his creatures.'

Now look at verse 21: 'Wherefore,' because God places such high value and importance upon his Word, 'lay apart all filthiness and superfluity of naughtiness, and receive with meekness the engrafted word, which is able to save your souls.'

If God has given you the privilege of hearing his Word, you should endeavour to profit as much as possible by it. The Word of the Lord is precious in these days. Those who have the blessed privilege of hearing it must not take that privilege lightly. When we come together with God's saints into the house of God, we should always come with the hope and expectation that we may meet God in his house and hear him speak. Whenever we come into the house of the Lord, our hearts should be filled with joy, gratitude and praise. But, at the same time, we should be aware that it is an awesome thing to come before the living God, even to worship (Eccles. 5:1-7). How we ought to admire and reverence the Word and worship of our God! Even Moses, the man of God, was required to take off his shoes when he stood before the Lord.

Whenever we come into the house of God we should 'take heed how [we] hear' (Luke 8:18). We are to remember *who God is*, the holy, eternal, almighty, just, incomprehensible God, Father, Son and Holy Spirit. Let a sense of his august being fill our hearts with reverence (Isa. 6:1-8). We must ever remember *what we are*, fallen, depraved, sinful worms, deserving of nothing but wrath from God. A sense of what we are should fill our hearts with humility (Eccles. 5:1-2). We should ever remember *what God has done for us* by his great grace. He devised a way of salvation for sinful men and women, and carried it out. God gave his dear Son to redeem and save us by the satisfaction of his justice through death (1 John 4:9-10). How we ought to love, adore and worship him! When we come into the house of God, we should be conscious that we are about to hear this great and gracious God speak to us. We are about to hear the living Word of the living God.

What a privilege! What a blessing! What a responsibility! The Son of God says, 'Blessed is the man that heareth me, watching daily at my gates, waiting at the posts of my doors' (Prov. 8:34). The apostle John wrote, 'Blessed is he that readeth, and they that hear the words of this prophecy, and keep those things which are written therein' (Rev. 1:3). Again, our Lord tells us that all who hear and obey the Word of God are as highly favoured of God as was Mary, who was chosen to be the instrument of his incarnation (Luke 11:27-28).

How can we hear the Word of God preached with the highest reverence and greatest profit to our souls? In our text the Spirit of God gives us three points of instruction about hearing the Word of God.

1. We must prepare ourselves to hear God's Word

This is something to be done before the sermon is preached. 'Wherefore lay apart all filthiness and superfluity of naughtiness' (v.21). If we desire to profit by the preaching of the gospel, we need to prepare our hearts to hear it with reverence.

How often we rush into the house of God without thought and preparation, as though we were late for an appointment which was not very important, with no more care than men have in going to a football match! May God both forgive and correct our irreverence!

Man, by nature, knows that he should give some reverence to God. But I am afraid that most of what appears to be reverence for God and his house is really nothing more than eagerness to have the approval of men. We take a bath, put on our best clothes, groom our hair and take great care to come to the house of God with respectable attire. And that is good. When men and women go to the house of God they should dress accordingly, modestly, neither overdressing nor underdressing. But there is something far more important than outward, physical appearance. We must prepare our hearts to hear from and worship God. Many of us may know that we should do so, but may not be sure how to prepare our hearts to hear the gospel.

James counsels us to *cleanse our hearts*: 'Lay apart all filthiness and superfluity of naughtiness.' The old prophet said, 'Rend your heart and not your garments.' When we come into the assembly of God's saints, we must take off the garments of earthly toil and care, wash away the filth of the day from our hearts and put on the garments of praise. As the priests of God, let us prepare ourselves to do service in the temple of God.

We are to *'lay aside all filthiness'*. Sin of every kind is debasing, filthy and offensive. By faith in Christ, by the grace of God, each of us must confess our sin to the Lord and lay it aside. We should bathe our souls in the laver of Christ's Word, his Spirit and blood, as we approach the altar of God.

When James uses the word 'filthiness' in this chapter, it is obvious that he is referring to three things in particular.

When we come into the house of God we must lay aside *the filth of covetousness* (v.11). Greed, worldly ambition, pride and the desire for gain are filthy things. If we would hear the Word of God with spiritual profit to our souls, we must separate ourselves from these things, asking God to remove our hearts from our natural tendency towards covetousness.

We must also lay aside *the filth of lust* (vv. 14-15). The indulgence of our animal passions (the lust of the flesh, the lust of the eye and the pride of life) makes us unfit to receive the pure Word of God. These lusts are so much a part of all men and women by nature that we must deliberately lay them aside when we come into the house of God, seeking the grace and power of his Spirit to subdue the lusts of our hearts.

We must lay aside *the filth of anger* (vv. 19-20). The God of peace will not be worshipped by men and women who are full of anger, wrath, malice and vengeance (Matt. 5:23-24). We must carefully avoid this snare of the devil. If he cannot keep us from the house of God, he will endeavour to keep us from hearing from God as we sit under the sound of the gospel, by filling our hearts with anger. Have you ever noticed how often and how easily we are provoked to anger when we are preparing to go to the house of God to hear the gospel? That is not accidental. Satan does not want us to profit by the Word. We must ever be 'swift to hear' God speak, 'slow to speak' against the message of God through his servant and 'slow to anger', slow to take offence at the Word spoken.

We can be sure that 'The wrath of man worketh not the righteousness of God.' Anything said, or done, in anger, wrath and malice is not the will of God and accomplishes nothing for the glory of God or the good of his people.

We must also lay aside 'all superfluity of naughtiness'. 'Naughtiness' is anything that keeps us from an entire submission to the Word of God, anything that interferes with our worship of, and devotion and consecration to, the Lord our God. Evil thoughts, earthly cares, carnal passions, petty quarrels, envy, jealousy, prejudice and strife are all included in that 'superfluity of naughtiness' which keeps men and women from receiving the Word of God.

If God has given you a faithful pastor, he earnestly labours to seek a message from God for you every time he stands to preach. He wants every message he preaches to be spiritually profitable to you. But his labour for you is in vain if his message is of no benefit to you. Therefore I urge you to prepare your heart to hear the gospel. Confess and forsake all that hinders you in worship. Seek the Lord.

Call upon him. Meditate upon his greatness, his goodness, his grace and his glory, upon your own sinfulness, weakness and need of that mercy which is found only in Christ. And remember that the preparation of your heart requires some preparation of your mind and body too, as we saw in the previous chapter.

2. We must receive the Word of God with the meekness of childlike faith

Here is something to be done during the sermon: 'Receive with meekness the engrafted Word, which is able to save your souls' (v. 21).

C. H. Spurgeon said, 'In the hearing of the Word there should be a receiving of it, not into the ear only, but into the understanding, into the heart, into the conscience, together with the laying up of this good treasure in the memory and the affections.'

Nothing can replace the preaching of the gospel. The man of God, standing in the place of God, with the authority of God, preaching the Word of God — this is the means which God has ordained for the accomplishment of his purposes, for the glory of his own great name and the eternal welfare of his people.

Gospel preaching is the means by which God saves his elect (Rom. 1:16: 10:17; 1 Peter 1:23-25).

Gospel preaching is the means by which God gives spiritual instruction and edification to the church of Christ (Eph. 4:11-16).

Gospel preaching is also the means by which Christ gives spiritual direction and exercises his rule in his spiritual kingdom, the church (Heb. 13:7, 17).

The preaching of the gospel is the one thing God has ordained as a means of grace. This is the one thing God will honour. This is the one thing by which the church of God will prevail. It must not be despised, neglected, or taken lightly. When we hear the gospel preached, we are to receive it with meekness. We cannot be saved unless we hear the gospel preached and receive it by faith.

We should, therefore, hear the Word of God *eagerly*. 'As newborn babes, desire the sincere milk of the Word, that ye may grow thereby' (1 Peter 2:2). Cornelius and those early Gentile believers were of the right mind. Cornelius said to Peter, 'Now therefore are we all here present before God, to hear all things that are commanded thee of God' (Acts 10:33). Imagine that—when the preacher arrived the people were already assembled and anxious to hear what God had to say by him! When Paul and Barnabas were at Antioch a good many Jews and Gentiles, having heard the glorious gospel of Christ, begged those messengers of grace to preach to them again (Acts 13:42-43). Because they were eager to hear the gospel, they heard it and profited by it.

We must make sure that we hear the Word of God *attentively*. When our Lord and his apostles first began to preach the gospel, the people hung upon their words, anxious to catch every syllable which fell from their lips. Is that how you listen to the Word of God? Do you remember how wonderful electing love, redeeming blood and saving grace sounded to your heart when you were first converted? Do you remember how your heart once leaped and danced, as you heard the preacher tell of free justification, imputed righteousness and absolute pardon in Christ, the sinner's substitute? Does it still thrill your heart and fill you with wonder? Something is wrong with that 'growth' which destroys astonishment. When I hear a man preach the gospel I want to be like a dry sponge, soaking up the dew of heaven like a sponge soaks up water.

We are to hear the preaching of God's holy Word with *reverence*. We are living in an age which tolerates, and even encourages, irreverence and disrespect for authority of any kind. But that must not be tolerated in the house of God. I am a pastor, and I speak as a pastor. The gospel I preach is the Word of God almighty. It is God's holy Word. I demand that it be respected as such. No one is welcome in the congregation I pastor who treats the Word of God, or the ministry of the Word, with the contempt of irreverence. Where the Word of the King is, there is power and authority. It commands awe and reverence.

Children must be taught to reverence the Word of God. They should not be allowed to disrupt any part of the ministry of the Word by running in and out of the service, fidgeting about, or playing with toys. Children, in our society, who are too young to sit still and listen to the Word should be kept in the nursery.

More importantly, the parents must themselves reverence the Word. If children see that their parents treat the ministry of the gospel with respect, they probably will do so too.

We are to hear the Word of God *believingly*. This is what James means by 'receiving' the word. It is to be received as the Word of

God, by faith, without question. If we do not receive the Word, upon its own authority, by faith, it will profit us nothing (Heb. 4:2). We must bow to and believe what God says about all things, particularly what he says about us and our sin, God and his holiness, Christ and his obedience, the Holy Spirit and his grace. Anyone who will not bow to the self-evident truths of God revealed in the gospel cannot be saved.

The Word of God must be received into a meek and submissive heart. 'Let every man be swift to hear, slow to speak, slow to wrath' (v. 19). Thomas Manton wrote, 'If we were as swift to hear as we are ready to speak, there would be less of wrath and more of profit in our meetings.'

Most people are anxious to tell what they know, or think they know, and what they think, and very slow to hear what God says. They weigh the Word of God in the balance with their own reason, religious tradition, experience and personal feeling. They dare to set themselves up as judges of the eternal God. Even in the house of public worship man tries to be the god of God!

I say plainly, no man will ever hear from God, worship God, or know God, until he bows to the authority of God's Word with a meek, teachable, believing spirit. Like young Samuel, our heart's attitude must be, 'Speak, Lord, thy servant heareth thee.' When we go to the house of God to hear a man preach the gospel, if we would profit by what we hear, we must be willing to have our faults exposed, take the rebuke and reproof of Holy Scripture, conform to the requirements of the Word, receive any doctrine taught in the Bible and forsake any doctrine, tradition, or practice not taught in the Word of God.

James has told us what to do before the sermon: 'Lay apart all filthiness and superfluity of naughtiness.' He has told us what to do during the sermon: 'Receive with meekness the engrafted Word.' Then he gives us the reason for doing so: this Word of God, which by the gospel is preached unto us, 'is able to save [our] souls'. The Word of God is the seed of life, miraculously and supernaturally implanted in the heart in regeneration, producing life and faith in God's elect by the power of his effectual, irresistible grace (Heb. 4:12; James 1:18; 1 Peter 1:23). We must receive the Word of God with meek, reverent, submissive hearts, because the eternal salvation of our immortal souls depends upon it!

3. We must obey the Word of God

This is something to be done after the sermon is over: 'Be ye doers of the word, and not hearers only, deceiving your own selves.' It is not enough to be charmed by the preacher's speech, astounded by his learning, impressed with his logic and stirred by his stories. It is not enough to hear the Word and say 'Amen' to all that we hear. If we would be saved by the gospel, we must obey the gospel. As Richard Baxter said, 'There must be an inward practice by meditation and an outward practice by obedience.' We must put into practice what we hear from God. It is not enough to say, 'I believe the Word of God!' We must do what God says. Otherwise, our religion is a vain pretence by which we deceive ourselves (James 1:23-25).

If we are wise, we will endeavour to retain what we hear. 'We ought to give the more earnest heed to the things which we have heard, lest at any time we should let them slip' (Heb. 2:1). We all have problems remembering important things. So we make notes to jog our memories. Certainly, nothing in this world is more important than a message from the eternal God! Therefore I recommend doing all you can to remember the Word preached to you. Take notes on what you hear. Meditate upon it. Discuss the message with others, and as soon as you have digested it, tell someone what you have heard.

We must make it our business to obey God's Word. Those who hear the Word of God and do not obey it will soon cease to hear God speak (Heb. 4:7). In the last day God will pour out the greatest measure of his wrath upon those who have heard, but wilfully refuse to obey the gospel of his free grace in Christ, 'the perfect law of liberty'. We must repent of our sin, trust the Lord Jesus Christ and surrender to the claims of Christ in the gospel. In all things we must seek to walk in and do the will of God.

If God has given you the blessed privilege of living in a place where you can hear the gospel of his free and sovereign grace in Christ faithfully proclaimed, cherish the privilege he has given you and thank him for it. Endeavour to profit as much as you can from every message your pastor preaches, and make your calling and election sure. Do not be deceived with a mere form of religion. In all things, make your rule of faith and conduct the Word of God alone.

16.
What should the church be?

'These things write I unto thee, hoping to come unto thee shortly: but if I tarry long, that thou mayest know how thou oughtest to behave thyself in the house of God, which is the church of the living God, the pillar and ground of the truth' (1 Tim. 3:14-15).

Our Lord has established two institutions in this world for the happiness and holiness of his people. First, he established the *home*. Before sin entered into the world, the Lord God saw that it was not good for man to dwell alone, so he made Adam a wife, a helpmeet for him, to be his companion (Gen. 2:18-24). God himself brought Adam and Eve together as husband and wife, and the first home was formed. Therefore it is written, 'Marriage is honourable in all, and the bed undefiled' (Heb. 13:4). Marriage is honourable among all people, and in marriage the bed is undefiled. Marriage is ordained of God for the happiness of men, the moral stability of society and the propagation of the race. Among men in this world nothing is sweeter, happier and more comforting than home. Home is not the house in which a family lives. Home is the family itself. Home is not a geographical location, but the people who live there and make up the household. Whenever they are together, that is home. I pity the man who does not enjoy the blessedness of a happy, peaceful, loving home!

Secondly, the Lord established his *church*, the church of the living God. When Peter had made his confession, 'Thou art the Christ, the Son of the living God', our Lord said, 'Upon this rock I will build my church; and the gates of hell shall not prevail against it' (Matt. 16:16, 18). This second institution, the church of the living God, is even more precious, more needful and more important than the first. That may seem strange, even offensive to some. But the family of God is more important than our personal families. Our Lord gave the church this priority by his own example (Mark 3:31-35). Our spiritual family is more important than our physical families. The house of God must be preferred to our own households. The cares and needs of God's church must take priority over the cares and needs of our own families.

Why is the church of God more important to a believer than his own family? It is because Christ loved the church, chose the church, redeemed the church, builds the church, honours the church and preserves the church. The church, the family of God, is an ever-lasting family. Our earthly families are only temporary; our spiritual family is eternal; and that which is eternal is more important than that which is temporal.

Think about the church, the family of God. Particularly, think about that local church of which you are a member. That is the subject of the text which heads this chapter. Paul's purpose in 1 Timothy was to instruct the young pastor, Timothy, and us, in the affairs of the church. He tells Timothy how to discharge honourably his office as a minister, evangelist, pastor and teacher in the house of God. He is teaching us how we are to behave in the house of God, as members of the family of God, and he is telling us what every local church should be. Every local church is 'the house of God, which is the church of the living God, the pillar and ground of the truth'. The church of God is a spiritual kingdom, a royal family, whose one purpose and design in this world is to uphold, maintain and set forth the truth of God.

In answering this question, 'What should the church be?' I will first make a practical observation, second, explain Paul's doctrine in the text and, third, issue a challenge to my readers.

1. A practical observation

I draw this observation both from the Word of God and from personal experience. It is an observation which both pastors and church members need to learn and remember: there never has been a perfect church upon this earth, nor will there ever be.

Frequently, I see people going from one church to another, seeking a church which measures up to their ideas of a perfect church. But their pursuit is vain. Pastors are often frustrated and depressed, and often move from one church to another, because the church does not measure up to their expectations. Churches are made up of sinful human beings, just like you and me. Therefore they have many faults.

In the kingdom of heaven tares and wheat grow together. As we have seen earlier, wherever the Lord sows wheat, Satan sows tares. Wherever the Lord gathers sheep, Satan herds his goats. Wherever you find grain in the field, you will find some chaff. God in his wisdom has ordained that it be so, for as long as time shall stand, and our Lord commands us to make no effort to separate the goats from the sheep, the tares from the wheat, or the chaff from the grain (Matt. 13:30). That is his job, and he is the only one capable of doing it. Any time pastors, elders, deacons and churches take it upon themselves to 'purge' the church, they do far more harm than good. Our judgement is so poor that we beat the sheep and pet the goats, pull up the wheat and leave the tares, and burn the grain and save the chaff.

We must not ignore the need for church discipline when it arises, but discipline is not for the purging of the church. Discipline is for the correction and restoration of the Lord's children, and the discipline of God's house is primarily carried out by the preaching of the gospel.

The churches of the New Testament had many, many problems, just like churches have today. When people talk about returning to 'New Testament Christianity', as though the churches then were better than the churches of the twentieth century, they reveal great ignorance. The first church had Judas for its treasurer. The church at Jerusalem was racially prejudiced. The church at Corinth was plagued with strife, division, incest, disorderly worship and drunkenness at the Lord's Table! The church in Galatia was nearly destroyed by legalism. And all the early churches of the New Testament era were assailed constantly by false brethren, false prophets and false doctrine from within.

Every local church today will experience the same kind of troubles from time to time. If the church of which you are a member is blessed of God with doctrinal stability, unity of the Spirit and brotherly love, if God has given spiritual peace and prosperity through the preaching of the gospel and keeps his people from shameful, outward acts of gross sin, you are truly blessed of God. You have much for which to be thankful. There are few such churches in this world. But if Satan should disrupt the church for a while, do not be shocked, and when trouble comes do not forsake your family. Faithful brethren will not forsake their family in time of need.

2. Paul's doctrine in this text

I want us to see what Paul says in this text about the church. In doing so, we shall see that he states again many of the truths which we learned in our earlier study of his address to the Ephesian elders.

Look at *the name Paul gives to the church.* He calls it 'the church of the living God'. What is the church? It is a congregation of believing people, gathered in the name of Christ, by the power and grace of the Holy Spirit, to worship God and obey his will. The church is a spiritual family, not a denominational organization.

The church belongs to God. It is not my church, your church, or our church. It is the Lord's church. He chose it. He bought it. He saved it. He owns it (Eph. 5:25-27).

It is the church of the living God. The church is the living body of Christ, her living Head. No one is truly a part of the church who is not united in a living relationship to the Lord Jesus Christ. The very worst thing that can happen to any local church is the decay of life. We must earnestly strive to avoid formalism, coldness and death. Spiritual life depends upon the Spirit of God. We must have more than a sound creed. We must have more than a proper form of worship. We must have the Spirit of God. A local church without the Spirit of God is like a body without a soul — dead, useless, decaying and obnoxious. The sooner it is buried the better.

The church is called 'the house of God'. What does Paul mean by such language? John Gill suggests that he means three things.

1. *The church is a spiritual house.* It is built of living stones, men and women who are born of God. It is built upon a sure foundation, the Lord Jesus Christ himself (1 Cor. 3:11). It is a house with one door of entrance, which is Christ, and two windows, the ordinances of the gospel — baptism and the Lord's Supper. And the pillars of this house are those men whom God has chosen to preach the gospel in it.

2. *The church is a family,* the family of God, the household of faith. This family is called by the name of Christ, the Master of the household. Within the family there are fathers, young men and children. The ministers of Christ, the servants of God, are the stewards of the family and the family is regulated by the law of Christ, love and trust.

3. *The church is the house of God,* the house which he builds, for which he provides, which he protects, in which he dwells. When men and women come together in the name of Christ, trusting his blood and righteousness, seeking his glory, seeking his will, to worship God, the triune God meets with them (Matt. 18:20). If the church of which you are a member is a true, New Testament church, that church, when it is gathered, is the house and temple of the living God (1 Cor. 3:16-17). The local church is the place where God is worshipped, wherever it is. It is the place of God's abode, the place where God reveals himself in Christ, the place of God's rule and the object of all his purposes and works. The church of the living God needs no priests, altars, rituals and none of the outward symbols of religion, but only God himself.

Are we of the house of God? If so, then let us be an obedient, reverent, grateful, worshipping, loving people. Let us honour our Father in all things!

Next, Paul tells us that *the church is 'the pillar and ground of the truth'*. The church, the local church, is the pillar which upholds, maintains and sets forth the truth. The church, the local church, is the ground which is the undergirding, stabilizing force of the truth.

The whole church, not just the pastor, elders, deacons and teachers, but the whole church and every member of it, is the pillar and ground of the truth. In the church of the living God the truth is constantly uplifted as a light in the midst of darkness. The church of God is the lighthouse of truth in this world. The one purpose and business of the church is to uphold, maintain and spread abroad the truth of God as it is in Christ Jesus. All her strength, all her talents, all her resources are to be given to and used for this one glorious work. Whatever God puts in our hands, whatever doors of opportunity are opened before us, all are to be used for the preaching of the gospel. Nothing is to be wasted upon any other cause.

There are other important causes in the world. But in God's providence, he raises up other people and organizations to take care of those causes. The church must not be turned aside from her far more important work. Members of political parties will support their politicians. Let God's church support gospel preachers. Doctors build hospitals and practise medicine. Let the church of Christ build churches and practise missions. Moralists will struggle for moral issues. Let the church struggle for the furtherance of the gospel. Educators will teach children the 'three Rs' of reading, writing and arithmetic. Let the church teach sinners the 'three Rs' of gospel truth — Ruin by the Fall, Redemption by the blood and Regeneration by the Holy Spirit. We have no other work. Let us uphold, proclaim and defend the truth of God with all our might. Truth is what we have received from our forefathers, truth is what we must maintain and truth is the legacy we must leave to the generations to come.

3. A challenge to the reader

If you are privileged to be a member of the house of God, a part of the church of the living God, which is the pillar and ground of the truth, then make it your business to maintain, defend and publish abroad the truth of God with every fibre of your being. See to it that the church to which you belong is 'the pillar and ground of the truth'. Any church which ceases to be a pedestal of the truth ceases to be a church.

Every believer must be engaged in this noble cause. The church of Christ must not tolerate in her pulpit any man who is opposed to, or indifferent to the truth.

We must not tolerate any attack upon, violation of, or compromise of the Word of God. The Bible alone is the inspired, inerrant, infallible Word of God. It is our only rule of faith and practice (Isa. 8:20; 2 Tim. 3:16-17). The Word of God alone is our creed, confession of faith and rule. We must bow to the authority of God's book, but only to the authority of God's book.

We must not tolerate any departure from the old paths of gospel truth (Jer. 6:16; 2 Tim. 1:8-13). Without hesitation or apology, we must sound out the glorious message of God's free, sovereign, eternal grace in Christ. We do not need to clarify the gospel, reform the gospel, or modernize the gospel. We need only to proclaim it. Let us proclaim the naked gospel, with all its barbs and rough edges. It is the power of God unto salvation to all who believe. We must especially proclaim those points of gospel truth against which men most naturally and constantly rebel. Lest any reader should mistake my meaning, I will state plainly, though briefly, what those points of gospel truth are which the church of God is responsible to proclaim in every generation.

1. *Divine sovereignty* (Rom. 9:11-24). If there is a God in heaven, he is absolutely sovereign over all things in creation, in providence, and, especially, in salvation.

2. *Total depravity* (Rom. 5:12; Eph. 2:1-3). Unless man is totally depraved by nature and utterly incapable of doing anything towards his own salvation, the death of Christ and the gospel of his grace are vain and useless.

3. *Unconditional election* (Eph. 1:3-6; 2 Thess. 2:13). If God has a people in this world whom he loves and to whom he is gracious, he loved them and determined to be gracious to them in eternal election, before the world was made. The immutable God changes not!

4. *Limited atonement* (Isa. 53:8; Heb. 2:17; 9:12). If the Lord Jesus Christ died to redeem sinners, then those sinners for whom he died are effectually and eternally redeemed. He cannot fail! Both the justice of God and the merits of Christ demand the eternal salvation of his people.

5. *Irresistible grace* (Ps. 65:4). If God the Holy Spirit sets out to save a sinner, that sinner will be saved by omnipotent, irresistible, effectual grace. When he draws, he fetches. When he calls, sinners come. His will cannot be thwarted. His grace cannot be resisted. His power cannot be defeated.

6. *Perseverance of the saints* (John 10:27-30). Every believing sinner will be preserved unto eternal glory, kept by the power of God. Not one of those chosen by God, redeemed by Christ and called by the Spirit can be lost.

And we must not tolerate any distortion of the ordinances of the gospel. Let us be sure that the ordinances of baptism and the Lord's Supper are observed according to the teaching of Scripture and that we do not substitute any practice which in the slightest degree casts doubt on the perfect holiness of Christ's person or the necessity of atonement by his death, burial and resurrection as our substitute.

Make certain that the church to which you belong is indeed 'the pillar and ground of the truth', and, being a part of such a church, give yourself entirely to the blessed work of upholding, maintaining and proclaiming the truth of God, for the glory of God. Use everything God puts in your hand for this glorious work and you will serve God, his church and your generation well.

17.
Why should we support missionaries?

'Which have borne witness of thy charity before the church: whom if thou bring forward on their journey after a godly sort, thou shalt do well: because that for his name's sake they went forth, taking nothing of the Gentiles. We therefore ought to receive such, that we might be fellow-helpers to the truth' (3 John 6-8).

The only proper reason for the existence of any local church in this world is the furtherance of the gospel. The church exists on earth only for the preaching of the gospel of the Lord Jesus Christ. The church of God is a sounding board for the gospel. It is our responsibility to use every means at our disposal to proclaim the gospel of Christ as fully and universally as we possibly can to the generation in which we live. We have no other commission (Matt. 28:18-20; Mark 16:15-16; Luke 24:46-48; Acts 1:8). One of the most effective means we have of preaching the gospel, in any age, is gospel missions, sending out missionaries to preach the good news of redemption and grace in Christ around the world.

When I first moved to Danville, Kentucky, and assumed the pastoral responsibilities of Grace Baptist Church, before we had a house of worship, before we began any other work, before the church was able to support the pastor as they desired, I asked the men and women of Grace Church to make a commitment to the support of gospel missionaries. We had no visible means of doing so. But I was convinced then, as I am now, that where there is a will to give God will supply the ability to give. As in all other things, our people rallied to their pastor's request. (Some of those saints make great personal sacrifices to support their pastor, those faithful men who preach the gospel in foreign countries and needy pastors and churches in our own country. I cannot sufficiently express my thanks to God for them, or commend them too highly.) Today it is our privilege to assist in the regular support of six faithful missionaries and their families, and we have never lacked anything needed for the work at home.

God honours those who honour him, and our congregation has been blessed of God, greatly blessed, since the day we began supporting these missionaries. We have lost nothing, but gained much, as our Lord promised (Luke 6:38).

In the future I intend to call upon myself and our church family to make greater sacrifices, to give more and do more for the cause of Christ, so that any man whom God raises up to preach the gospel of Christ anywhere in the world will not lack material support for his family. I call upon my readers to do the same. Why? Why do I ask for such commitment? Why do I call upon God's people to give to missions? Why should we support missionaries? In this chapter I want to give some plain, biblical answers to that question.

What is a missionary?

First let me clearly define what a missionary is. The word 'missionary' is not used in the Bible, but that should not disturb us. Neither is the word 'Trinity'. We practise missions, as we believe the doctrine of the Trinity, because the concept is clearly taught. The biblical word for missionary is 'evangelist'. Paul and Barnabas were missionaries sent out from the church at Antioch to preach the gospel to the Gentiles (Acts 13:1-3). Philip the evangelist was a missionary (Acts 21:8). All pastors are to do the work of an evangelist, or missionary (2 Tim. 4:5). But God has given some to his church who are specifically called to be missionaries or evangelists (Eph. 4:11).

A missionary is a man. No woman can serve as an evangelist, for an evangelist is a preacher and God does not call women to preach the gospel (1 Cor. 14:35; 1 Tim. 2:11-12). The wife of a missionary, that is, of an evangelist, is not herself a missionary in the true sense of the word, however much she may be an excellent wife to her husband, any more than the fact of being the wife of the President makes the First Lady herself the President of the United States.

A missionary is a man with God's message. First and foremost, like every other man called to the work of the gospel, the missionary is a preacher. If a man is not gifted to preach, he cannot serve as a missionary. And the message he preaches is, and must be, the gospel of God's free and sovereign grace in Christ. The missionary is a proclaimer of good news; and the good news he proclaims is the redemption Christ accomplished for sinners.

A missionary is a man with God's mission. Missionaries are men called and gifted of God to establish churches, train pastors and help establish those pastors and churches in the gospel of the grace of God, so that they might carry on the work of the gospel for the years to come. Medical missionaries, educational missionaries and cultural missionaries are not true missionaries and should not be supported by local churches. Missionaries are men who have a mission from God, and their mission is to preach the gospel of Christ.

With these things in mind, I want us to examine what the Spirit of God teaches in 3 John about the church's responsibility to missionaries. Here is a letter written by the apostle John to his beloved son in the faith, Gaius. Gaius was not a pastor, preacher, or elder. He was a man whom God had saved, a believer, a member of a local church, which had been visited by some missionaries. These missionaries were travelling about, preaching the gospel to the Gentiles. In their journeys they stopped at the town where Gaius lived, to visit the brethren there. So Gaius took them into his house, fed them, entertained them and lodged them for several days, perhaps for several weeks, and when they left he gave them some travelling money to help with their expenses. When they got back to the church of which John was the pastor, these travelling evangelists, these missionaries, could not stop talking about Gaius. They told John about him. They told their friends about him. They told the whole church about Gaius. When John heard these men talking about his spiritual son, his heart bubbled up with joy and gratitude. He wrote this letter, by the inspiration of God the Holy Spirit, to commend Gaius. And he does commend him! He tells us that Gaius loved the gospel (vv. 3-4), that he was faithful in all things (v. 5), and that he was generous, charitable and hospitable to his brethren, even to those who were total strangers (vv. 5-6). Like Abraham, Gaius entertained strangers who came to him in the name of Christ, and in so doing, he entertained angels unawares (Gen. 18:3; Heb. 13:2).

After highly commending this man, Gaius, for all that he had done, John urged him to do even more. Realizing that God's servants are to be supported entirely by the generous, free, voluntary gifts of his people, John gave Gaius, and us, four reasons why we should support missionaries.

1. It is pleasing to God for us to do so

John told Gaius that when God's servants come to our town, we are not only to care for them while they are with us, but we are to 'bring [them] forward on their journey after a godly sort' (v. 6).

It is the responsibility of local churches to provide all those things which God's servants need to carry on their work. Missionaries have all the earthly needs that the rest of us have and many that we do not have. They must have homes, food and clothing for their families. They must provide health care for their households. They have to educate their children, and they have to have some means of transport, just like we do. In addition to these things, every expense for the work on the field comes out of the missionary's pocket! Whatever it takes to keep faithful men free of earthly care, so that they may give themselves whole-heartedly to the work of the ministry, we must do!

John tells us that this is a 'godly sort' of work. The marginal translation of these words is: this is a work 'worthy of God'. It is a work becoming to those who serve God. If we do this, if we support God's servants in the work of the gospel, we do well. This is a work pleasing to God. God delights to see those who love Christ showing their love by generosity towards his servants (2 Cor. 9:7).

2. We should give 'for his name's sake'

'For his name's sake they went forth' (v.7). And 'for his name's sake' we must supply their needs.

There is only one thing that compels the true servant of God to take his wife and children to a remote, far distant country, to preach the gospel, leaving behind the comforts of his homeland, the company of his friends and the warmth of his family: he is motivated by a burning jealousy for the name of Christ (Rom. 1:5, 16, 17). That same burning jealousy for Christ's name inspires God's saints to give of their means to supply those men with the support they need. Every believer wants all men and women to hear the gospel of Christ, so that our great Saviour may be known, trusted, worshipped and glorified throughout the world. The best means we have of accomplishing that great goal is giving of our means to support faithful gospel-preaching missionaries.

Our Lord is so highly honoured by the service of those whom he sends out to preach the gospel that he counts anything we do for them as having been done for him (Matt. 10:40-42), and indeed it is. God's servants are his ambassadors. Those men who faithfully preach the gospel of God's free and sovereign grace in Christ (the gospel of his electing love, accomplished redemption, effectual grace and saving fulness) are God's representatives and spokesmen in this world (2 Cor. 5:18-21). Anything we do to one of God's ambassadors we do to him. Anything done for God's ambassador is done for him; and anything done against God's ambassador is done against him.

3. Faithful men have no other means of support

'Because that for his name's sake they went forth, taking nothing of the Gentiles' (v. 7). These men preached to the Gentiles freely, refusing to seek, or even take financial support from unbelievers.

There are three things I want to say about preachers and money. I know what the people of this world think, and I know that the preachers of this world have a terrible reputation regarding money. Preachers, as a whole, are the poorest credit risks in our society. They have a terrible reputation for living beyond their means and not paying their bills. That is horribly shameful! But we must never make the mistake of stereotyping God's servants with the characteristics of religious hirelings. God's servants are worthy of our generous support. Because they are faithful to Christ, the gospel of his grace and the souls of men, they have no means of support other

than the generosity of God's people. There are three things we need
to know about God's servants.

1. *God's servants do not preach for earthly gain.* These men described by John 'went forth, taking nothing of the Gentiles'. They
did not go out seeking men's goods. They went forth seeking men's
souls. It is never hard to tell whether a preacher is seeking your
goods, or the good of your soul. If he spends the bulk of his time
talking about your goods (health, wealth and prosperity), you can be
sure the rogue is after your money! If he spends his time and energy
speaking to you about Christ and your soul, it is because he is
seeking the good of your soul.

Paul condemned those pretentious, self-motivated, covetous,
greedy false prophets who make merchandise of men's souls and
prostitute the gospel for gain (2 Cor. 2:17; 1 Thess. 2:5-9). God's
servants do not seek personal gain. They will not enrich themselves by
the gospel. It would be impossible to make a faithful pastor or
missionary rich. If he is faithful, that which he does not need he will give
to someone who does. He has no desire to hoard up money, lands or
jewels. Can you imagine a rich prophet or apostle? Ridiculous!

2. *Our Lord expressly forbids his servants to solicit support,
especially from unbelievers.* When he sent his disciples out to
preach, he said, 'Go not from house to house' (Luke 10:7). That
means, 'Do not go begging, soliciting help, or in any way implying
that the cause of Christ, his church, his gospel, or his servants
depend upon the aid and support of men.

If I am God's servant, material, monetary, earthly consider-
ations have nothing to do with what, where, when, or how I preach.
In over twenty years of preaching, I have never asked anyone for a
penny, nor even allowed the consideration of cost or expense to
enter into any decision regarding the work of the ministry. I am
God's servant, and God meets my needs. The church I pastor is
God's church, and God supplies our needs. We will not dishonour
our heavenly Father by begging and grovelling before men for a
little money. I write from personal experience, but what I have said
is true of all who truly serve our God. Any man who begs for money
in the name of Christ, promising rewards from God if people give
him their money, or implying that God's work might fail if they do
not, is a liar and a false prophet.

3. *The Lord Jesus also forbids his servants to make provision for themselves* (Matt. 10:9-10; Luke 10:4-7). God's servants should not have to provide for themselves, and it is wrong for local churches to make it necessary for them to do so by being, selfish, niggardly misers. No servant of God, no man who truly ministers to the souls of men, should be required to provide even a piece of bread for himself or his family. It is the responsibility of local churches to take care of those who preach the gospel and to see that those who preach the gospel live by the gospel. The less earthly care a pastor or missionary has, the freer he is to give himself to the work of the ministry (prayer, study, preaching, writing, etc.); and the more he gives himself to these things, the more useful he is in the cause of Christ.

Not only is this the responsibility of local churches; it is what God's churches in fact do. God's saints are not misers! If God is in any work, anywhere in the world, God will supply the needs of that work through the free, voluntary, generous gifts of his people. Anything that has to be primed, pumped, pushed, pulled and promoted by men is not of God.

4. By our loving, free generous support of God's faithful servants, we become 'fellow-helpers to the truth' (v. 8)

When we supply a man's needs, so that he can preach the gospel of Christ freely to others, we become allies with him in the work of preaching the gospel. What a privilege! The work of the ministry is God's work, but God does his work through the labours of faithful men, through the preaching of the gospel. And these men do their work by the generosity of faithful men and women, who work hard and freely give of their means, so that the gospel may be preached freely around the world.

God's church is one, and we are one with those missionaries we are privileged to support. Their cause is our cause; their work is our work, and their reward is our reward.

The next time we have the opportunity to show hospitality to, entertain, give to, or do anything for, one of God's servants, let us remember these things:

1. This is a work that is pleasing to God.

2. This is a work that is done by faith in and for the honour of Christ's name.

3. This is a work done for worthy men, men who have forsaken all to preach the gospel. They are worthy to live by the gospel.

4. By these things we are 'fellow-helpers to the truth'.

Let each one of us do whatever God gives us the opportunity and the ability to do for Christ, his servants and the furtherance of the gospel, and let us pray that God will continue to raise up men to preach the gospel of his free grace in the Lord Jesus Christ for the salvation of his elect and the glory of his own great name. 'The harvest truly is great, but the labourers are few: pray ye therefore the Lord of the harvest, that he would send forth labourers into his harvest' (Luke 10:2).

18.
The financial support of the gospel ministry

'Let him that is taught in the word communicate unto him that teacheth in all good things. Be not deceived; God is not mocked: for whatsoever a man soweth, that shall he also reap. For he that soweth to his flesh shall of the flesh reap corruption; but he that soweth to the Spirit shall of the Spirit reap life everlasting. And let us not be weary in well doing: for in due season we shall reap, if we faint not. As we have therefore opportunity, let us do good unto all men, especially unto them who are of the household of faith' (Gal. 6:6-10).

No study of the local church and the believer's responsibilities to it would be complete if it did not address the matter of pastoral support. The material, financial support of gospel preachers is the subject Paul deals with in Galatians 6:6-10.

The fact is, every local church needs money to operate. Buildings must be erected. Bills must be paid. Office supplies must be purchased. Equipment must be maintained and salaries must be paid. We are to preach the gospel freely to all men, seeking nothing in return, but in order for us to preach the gospel freely, someone has to pay for it. How is the work of the ministry to be maintained? How should local churches raise the money needed to support pastors, missionaries and various works for the furtherance of the gospel? These are the questions we shall examine in this chapter. They are questions which need to be answered plainly and frankly from the Word of God.

There is no scarcity of material in the Holy Scriptures regarding the financial support of the gospel ministry. It is a subject which appears again and again throughout the Bible.

Under the Mosaic economy of the Old Testament those who ministered about the holy things of divine service lived upon the things of the temple. Those who served the altar were partakers of the altar (1 Cor. 9:13). God prescribed by law that the priesthood, the children of Levi, should receive a tenth of all the possessions of the children of Israel, a tenth of their money, property, crops and herds, for their service in the tabernacle of the congregation. The Jews were required to pay a tithe to be used exclusively for the financial support of the ministry of the Levitical priesthood (Num. 18:21). Failure to do so, for any reason, was regarded as robbing God himself (Mal. 3:8-9).

However, we are not under the law today. God's people are no more required to pay a tithe in this gospel age than we are required to keep the sabbath day, or observe the Passover (Col. 2:16-23). We are free from the law. A. D. Muse, the late pastor of Hearts Harbor Tabernacle in Louisville, Kentucky, used to say, 'If you tithe, you're under the law. And if you don't tithe you're an outlaw.' In other words, the person who just pays his tithe is a mere legalist; and anyone who does not do that much is an antinomian. Anyone who uses his freedom from the law as an excuse for being a niggardly miser and selfishly refuses to give of his means for the support of the gospel of Christ is, I fear, without grace. God's people give. They give generously, and they give cheerfully.

The instructions given in the New Testament regarding the financial support of the gospel ministry are unmistakably clear. Those men and women who believe the gospel of the grace of God are expected to support generously those who preach it. Not only is this expected; among God's saints it is practised. God's children are not miserly, self-centred worldlings. They are stewards who use what God has put in their hands for the cause of Christ. They need only to be instructed from the Word of God, and they gladly submit to it.

Our Lord Jesus Christ tells us plainly and repeatedly that those who preach the gospel are to live by the gospel (Matt. 10:9-10; Luke 10:4-7; 1 Cor. 9:14; 1 Tim. 5:17-18). Those men who faithfully preach the gospel of God's free and sovereign grace in Christ are to be supported and maintained by the people to whom they minister.

Faithful missionaries should be as fully and generously supported by the churches that send them out as the pastors of those local churches.

There were times when Paul and his companions were required to make tents to support themselves in the work of the gospel. It was an honourable thing for them to do so. Paul tells us that his goal was not to enrich himself, but to avoid being a burden to young churches (1 Thess. 2:9) and to avoid causing an offence to young, weak believers (1 Cor. 9:15-19). But the fact that God's messenger had to spend his time and efforts making tents was a shameful reproach upon the churches. Those churches that were established in the gospel should have assumed the responsibility of supplying Paul's needs and the needs of his companions, as they travelled from place to place preaching the gospel. The New Testament clearly makes it the responsibility of every local church to provide for the financial, material support of those who preach the gospel of Christ.

This is Paul's subject in Galatians 6:6-10. Here, by the inspiration of God the Holy Spirit, the apostle of Christ gives us three points of instruction in the matter of churches supporting those who preach the gospel.

1. A reasonable precept

'Let him that is taught in the word communicate unto him that teacheth in all good things' (v. 6). This is one of the clearest statements in the Bible about the support of gospel preachers. All who profit from the preaching of the gospel are expected to give of their means for the support of those who preach the gospel.

The word 'communicate' means 'to share with or distribute to'. It comes from the word 'communion' and basically means the same thing as 'fellowship'. Paul is saying, 'Let everyone to whom the gospel is preached have fellowship with and participate in the preaching of the gospel by supplying the earthly, material needs of those who preach it.'

To whom is this communication to be made?

Paul did not lay down a blanket rule that we should give financial support to every preacher, evangelist, or missionary who comes

along, claiming to speak for God. Those who deny the gospel of
Christ, preachers of free-will, works religion, are not to be supported
by God's saints (2 John 9-11).

Paul's doctrine is this: those preachers who faithfully teach the
Word of God are to be supported by the church; particularly, they are
to be supported by the churches they pastor. We must not let
ourselves be deceived by personality, charm or flowery speech.
God's prophets are not always personable, but they are always
profitable. Their delivery is not always impressive, but their message is always instructive. Their preaching is not always stirring, but
it is always sound. Every preacher must be judged by one thing:
what does he preach? What is his doctrine? God's servants faithfully
instruct men and women in the Word by preaching the gospel of
Christ. They teach their hearers the Word of truth; and those who
hear them are taught in the Word of truth. If a man is sent of God to
preach the gospel, he will preach with such unmistakable clarity that
all who hear him regularly will be taught the doctrine of Christ.

If you want to know what a man preaches, ask the people who
hear him. If he consciously and consistently preaches the gospel
they will know it (see John 18:19-21). It is impossible for a person
to hear a man preach the gospel regularly and not know, at least in
his head, the doctrine of the gospel. He will know his lost condition
of depravity and condemnation by nature (Rom. 5:12; Eph. 2:1-3).
He will have some understanding of the doctrine of Christ: our
Lord's divine person, his incarnation and virgin birth, his representative obedience to God for his people, his effectual, sin-atoning,
substitutionary death. Those who are privileged to hear a man
faithfully preach the gospel will know that salvation is by grace
alone through faith in Christ alone. All who hear the gospel
faithfully preached are taught what happened in the garden, what
happened on the cross, and how God saves sinners. And the man
who faithfully preaches those things is worthy of the financial
support of God's people.

*It is the responsibility of God's church to supply generously the
needs of every man who faithfully preaches the gospel of God's free
and sovereign grace in Christ.* This is only reasonable. Are you
taught the good things of the gospel? Then it is your reasonable and
equitable responsibility to supply the material needs of the man who
teaches you. You should supply him with good things materially,

who supplies you with good things spiritually (1 Cor. 9:11). It is the ordinance of Christ that 'They which preach the gospel should live of the gospel' (1 Cor. 9:14). No man who preaches the gospel of the grace of God should be required to provide for himself or his family (Acts 6:2-4; 2 Tim. 2:4). This support of the ministry must begin with each local church supporting its own pastor. Once that is taken care of, every local church should assume responsibility for the support of faithful missionaries. Those churches which are well established should also assist in the support of smaller churches and their pastors.

God's servants are not ambitious, greedy men. Faithful men will not abuse, or take advantage of, the generosity of God's people (1 Cor. 9:17-18). But God's preachers should never be expected to live as paupers. Those men who labour in the Word and doctrine of Christ, faithfully giving themselves to the work of the ministry, are to be supported generously in a comfortable life-style.

I am often asked, 'How much should the church pay its pastor?' I often reply, 'How much does it take for you to live?' The pastor has a wife and children to clothe, feed, house and educate, just like you. And he will incur many necessary expenses which you do not. His home is a virtual free hotel for God's people, and he wants it to be. His table almost always has a few extra mouths to feed, and he wants them there. He has miles to travel and books to buy, necessary for his work. All these things require cold, hard cash every week. When the church contemplates the pastor's salary a good rule of thumb is this: pay the pastor at least as much as the average income of the working men in the congregation, and then add enough to cover his additional expenses. If the church is not able to do what is needed, it is expected and responsible to do the best it can, and this is only reasonable.

How is this financial support to be secured?

This may seem strange to some, but the way to secure financial support for the gospel of Christ and those who preach it is in fact not to secure it. God will supply the needs of his church and his servants by the free, voluntary, generous gifts of his people. The moment a preacher, a missionary, or a church begins to secure its financial stability on its own, it leans upon the arm of the flesh and dishonours God.

There are some things, dishonouring to God and contrary to the gospel of his grace, which must not be done. God's church must never be brought back under the law, by having the law of the tithe imposed upon them. We must never solicit pledges from people, hold bake sales or rummage sales, or set up investment schemes to raise money for God's work. God's servants and his churches must never beg and grovel for help from men, as though the work of God depended upon man's assistance. Nor must we ever solicit the aid of unbelievers. I know these things are commonly practised in our day, but they are contrary to every principle of grace and faith. God's church operates by faith, and faith looks to God, not man! Any work that is of God will have its needs supplied by God through the free, voluntary gifts of God's saints (2 Cor. 9:7).

If a pastor wants the people to whom he preaches to be generous, he must be generous. In all things, like a shepherd, the pastor must lead God's sheep and show them the way by personal example. The moment men and women detect selfishness, greed and unfaithfulness in their pastor, these things will be reflected in them.

The Word of God supplies us with an abundance of instruction about this matter of giving. All of 1 Corinthians 9 and 2 Corinthians chapters 8-9 are taken up with this subject. But there are no commands given to the people of God, anywhere in the New Testament, about how much we are to give, when we are give, or where we are to give. Tithing and all systems like it are totally foreign to the New Testament. Giving, like all other acts of worship, is an act of faith and grace. It must be free and voluntary, or it is unacceptable. However, there are some plain, simple guidelines laid down in the Scriptures for us to follow. Here are ten things revealed in the New Testament about giving.

1. Our giving should be planned (2 Cor. 9:7).
2. Our giving must be free, voluntary, unconstrained (2 Cor. 9:7).
3. Our giving must be motivated by love and gratitude towards Christ (2 Cor. 8:7-9).
4. Our giving must arise from a willing heart (2 Cor. 8:12).
5. Every believer should give to the work of the gospel according to his personal ability (1 Cor. 16:2).

6. Every believer should give a portion of his goods for the cause of Christ (1 Cor. 16:2).

7. Our gifts for the gospel should be liberal and sacrificial (2 Cor. 9:5-6; Mark 12:41-44).

8. We are to give as unto the Lord (Matt. 6:1-5).

9. This kind of giving is well-pleasing to God (2 Cor. 9:7; Phil. 4:18; Heb. 13:16).

10. If we are willing to give, God will supply us with the ability to give (2 Cor. 9:10: Luke 6:38; Phil. 4:19).

Someone once said, 'There are three kinds of giving: grudge-giving, duty-giving and thanksgiving. Grudge-giving says, "I have to." Duty-giving says, "I ought to." Thanksgiving says, "I want to."'

2. A recognized principle

'Be not deceived; God is not mocked: for whatsoever a man soweth, that shall he also reap. For he that soweth to his flesh shall of the flesh reap corruption; but he that soweth to the Spirit shall of the Spirit reap life everlasting.'

'Be not deceived.' The Judaizers and false teachers at Galatia were persuading these men and women not to support the men who faithfully preached the gospel of Christ to them, and devised many excuses for them not to do so, which the Galatians readily seized. People are easily led astray from what they know to be right by personal greed and covetousness. They often excuse their miserliness by their own earthly cares and responsibilities, or by finding some petty fault with the preacher. Neither excuse is valid. If we work hard and live within our means, we will not be too financially tied to give. Nor do our personal likes or dislikes of something about God's messenger in any way lessen our responsibility to support him in the work of the gospel. Men with money often try to exert control over a pastor by how much they give, or refuse to give. It should not need saying that God's people do not have this attitude, or that God's servants cannot be controlled by money!

'God is not mocked.' Men and women who find excuses not to give to the cause of Christ and work of the gospel mock God. Paul is

saying, 'You cannot insult God and get away with it!' Remember, in the context Paul is talking about the support of the gospel ministry. If a man comes to you in the name of God, preaching the gospel of Christ, and you refuse to give of your means to support him, you insult God! And you will not get away with it!

'For whatsoever a man soweth, that shall he also reap.' This is a universal law, applying to every realm of life. Generally speaking, whatever we sow, as to kind, quality and quantity, we will reap. If a farmer sows wheat, he reaps wheat. If he sows sparingly, he will reap sparingly. If he sows bountifully, he will reap bountifully. If he sows good seed, he will reap a good harvest. If he sows nothing, he will reap nothing. Everyone understands that in the natural world, but here Paul applies it to the things of God.

'He that soweth to his flesh shall of the flesh reap corruption.' In other words, if we use what God puts in our hands to pamper our flesh and gratify our personal greed and covetousness, if we spend our substance upon luxuries for ourselves and our families, or hoard it up to increase our riches, we shall of the flesh reap corruption. Paul is telling us that the way we use, or abuse, our money reveals the true state and condition of our hearts (see Matt. 6:19-24).

'But he that soweth to the Spirit shall of the Spirit reap life everlasting.' This does not mean that men and women can earn salvation, or even a greater degree of heavenly reward and glory by what they give to the cause of Christ. The text simply means that, if we lay out our worldly substance for the cause of Christ, the preaching of the gospel and the good of his kingdom, we will reap that for which we have sown it — 'life everlasting'! Our use of what God puts in our hands does not secure anything for us, but it does reveal the true state and condition of our hearts (Matt. 25:24-30).

3. A required perseverance

'And let us not be weary in well doing: for in due season we shall reap, if we faint not. As we have therefore opportunity, let us do good unto all men, especially unto them who are of the household of faith.'

Satan uses many things to discourage us, and God uses many things to try us. We do not see immediate results. Our circumstances, the economy of the nation and the needs of our families all change. We sometimes begin to think, 'Maybe I ought to stop, or at least curtail my giving. Nothing much appears to be accomplished by it. The kingdom of God will get along all right without my few dollars in the offering plate.'

To such thoughts, Paul says, 'Don't give up now!' 'In due season,' at God's appointed time, 'we shall reap, if we faint not.' The seed sown will spring up again, and the bread cast upon the waters will be found after many days. But there must be a time of waiting, between the sowing of the seed and the reaping of the harvest. This time of waiting is to try our faith, to prove whether we really believe God. It is our responsibility to use what God has given us for the cause of Christ, to sow to the Spirit and to wait for God to give the increase. He will give it in his way, at his time, for his glory.

'As we have therefore opportunity, let us do good unto all men, especially unto them who are of the household of faith.' By doing good Paul means communicating to the needs of men and women, particularly to the needs of God's children, and in this context to the needs of his servants. While the time of life lasts, let us use what God gives us for the good of his people and the furtherance of the gospel. If we do so, then we partake of and have fellowship with God's servants in their work (Matt. 10:40-42).

I am calling for commitment to Christ. If I am committed to something, I throw my life into it; and if I am committed to the cause of Christ in this world, I throw my life into his cause. That means that I do whatever has to be done and give whatever has to be given to get the job done. The very least that I can do is give! As you come to the end of this book, I ask you to give yourself in unreserved commitment to Christ, the gospel of his grace and the church of God.